The Art Of Anchoring TV *&* Live *Events*

Bindiya Dutt

PUSTAK MAHAL®

Administrative office and sale centre

J-3/16 , Daryaganj, New Delhi-110002
☎ 23276539, 23272783, 23272784 • *Fax:* 011-23260518
E-mail: info@pustakmahal.com • *Website:* www.pustakmahal.com

Branches
Bengaluru: ☎ 080-22234025 • *Telefax:* 080-22240209
E-mail: pustak@airtelmail.in • pustak@sancharnet.in
Mumbai: ☎ 022-22010941, 022-22053387
E-mail: rapidex@bom5.vsnl.net.in
Patna: ☎ 0612-3294193 • *Telefax:* 0612-2302719
E-mail: rapidexptn@rediffmail.com

ISBN 978-81-223-1458-8

Edition: 2013

Printed at :Radha Offset, Delhi

Preface

Event and Television Anchoring are attractive businesses today. Fascinated by the glitz and glamour, many people keenly look at anchoring as a career option. With the boom in the Indian Television Industry there is an influx of talent from all over the world.

Charmed by a high flying lifestyle people often get inspired to move to big cities that are filled with work opportunities in Media to try their luck. Today, anchoring is viewed as a lucrative career option and several people flock to cities where the television industry exists. Though most national news channels have bureaus all over the country, Mumbai remains the hub of media in India. There are several regional and local channels, in different parts of the country. New Delhi also boasts of news and lifestyle channels but at the end of the day, most folks assemble in Mumbai to be a part of mainstream television. In large metros, apart from anchoring a lot of anchors get an opportunity to try modeling as well as acting.

Many aspirants arrive from the US, Canada, Australia and other parts of the globe to get a taste of the Television Industry in India. Seduced by glamour and fame several NRI's pack their dreams in their bags to explore a possibility of becoming an anchor.

Fame, glamour and money are great charmers that can trap like no one else. When viewed from a distance this work seems quite rewarding but when you take a closer look, you see a lot of loop holes. There is a pre-conceived notion that anchoring is a way to earn money easily. There is no such thing as easy money in any genuine business, and anchoring is no different. Well, that could be true sometimes but we will thoroughly get into the monetary aspect of it later. For starters let us explore the term "anchoring".

Though popularly known as Anchoring, it has many other names. Some call it Video Jockey (VJ), while others term it as Compere, Master of Ceremonies (MC), TV host or Presenter. Whichever name one chooses to use the work remains the same.

This book aspires to offer you with a clear understanding of the business of television and event anchoring. Whether or not you have gained any formal training in anchoring, this book will help you understand the business of anchoring. Whether you are originally from a city where television is big business or you have recently moved there from another city or country to find a work as an anchor, you will gain a fresh perspective from reading this book.

Though this book does not focus on news or journalism, it features some inferences derived from observations of newscasters and news channels. There are a few common factors that concern all anchors, whether news or entertainment which are highlighted. This work focuses mostly on entertainment and corporate anchoring and only mentions news as and when necessary.

The purpose of this book is to act as a guide and offer relevant tips for you to follow. This will validate your experiences and clarify any pre-conceived notions you may carry. The idea of this book is to assist people to gain knowledge of the entire business of anchoring before they step into it.

I wish I had a manual when I walked into my first audition. I have learned by trial and error but you don't have to. The intention is to offer you a road map and save your time. The idea is to shed light on the different facets of this business. The motive is to offer you information which is concrete and coherent. By the end of this book you will be more knowledgeable about this business and much happier that you got access to this information. There is a lot in store but for now let us take a sneak peek into the world of anchoring and explore the nuances of Event and TV anchoring. Before we begin to delve deeper, let's ask a few relevant questions.

Contents

Part 1

The Basics

1

Is Anchoring Meant For You?

There are many people today who aspire to take up anchoring as their profession. Most are neither professional journalist's nor do they have any formal training in public speaking. They just plunge into it without thinking much. Before jumping into the sea, it is important to either learn to swim or to ensure that once you jump in, there will be someone to rescue you so that you do not sink. In our careers, however, many a times we jump into something without having any prior knowledge. When we buy a new car, we usually do a test drive but before we get into a new venture, do we test the waters? Do we research the market? Do we ask people for advice? Do we gauge whether our nature coincides with that of the work that we intend to do? Many of us do not attempt to research what it really takes and without considering the aftermath, we jump into it only to later realize what we have gotten ourselves into. None of us can predict the future but if we want to make a sound decision, it is important to consider diverse aspects of any work that might interest us. So before plunging in, research what is going on in the business. I got into anchoring without any research. I did not test the waters, nor did I seek much advice from people. I chose the most popular trial-and-error method. Had I known then what I know now, it would have certainly helped. Before you take up anchoring, ask yourself if this is what you really want to do and if this work will suit you? To help you answer this question, there is a lot of insider's information here.

Many people I have known as co-anchors follow a premise that anchoring equals easy money where the stakes are not as high as other businesses. To an extent it may be true that the initial monetary investment is rather low and the returns are high, provided you know what you are doing. However, it is extremely important to understand that though the financial investment is much lower as compared to other start-up businesses, the mental investment is very high. The time that actors, models and anchors spend on looking for work is a lot more than what they actually spend on doing the work. Even after standing in audition lines for hours, many never see themselves on TV. With great difficulty and a lot of luck a few get selected as television anchors. In every nook and corner you will find good looking, well groomed, young, ambitious and hopeful faces who await their big break. The investment may not be evident but the stakes are very high. Why then there are so many young, vibrant, qualified people vying for the same job?

Fame is a great seducer, as most of us are aware. A lot of folks want to be seen and recognized and for that they are ready to give up a lot of what they have. There is a lot that people invest once they set out on this path. They invest their precious time, their hopes and dreams, their money and most importantly their mind.

Do not be fooled into believing that this work is easy. The actual work might not take a toll on you, but the process is rather tough. When you first begin, people want to see your pictures, so you need a portfolio. I have seen new people rolling into auditions without their pictures. They seem to think, "Why do you need my photos when I am present myself? I look better in person anyway." Well, they may have a point but they still have to present their portfolio, especially if they are auditioning for TV. Event anchors can get away without photographs. To many it comes as a surprise that even anchors need a portfolio. People often thought that portfolios were only meant for actors and models. If you are auditioning for TV, you need to show your professional photographs. That is the only way for casting directors to get a sense of how photogenic you are. So if you aspire to work in TV, you have to invest in a decent portfolio. You then need to go for auditions, meet people who can offer you work, get yourself some nice clothes, shoes, makeup and so on. You need to join a gym to keep fit, you need to eat healthy and maintain a certain look. Think of all that you will give up for this work. If you are from out of town or country, chances are that you are giving up your luxurious lifestyle. You have to find accommodation, you have to eat outside food (unless you cook or have hired a cook), you have to stay in great health despite the fact that you may not have access to the most hygienic food at all times. Additionally, you have to spend time and money on long commutes, you have to always look good, you have to stand in long lines waiting to be auditioned, you have to bear with the day to day hassles, uncertainties, rejections, disappointments and to add fuel to the fire, you still are not guaranteed work. Now that's a catch! However, the illusions of fame are so strong that people are ready to overlook the negative aspects of the job and put everything else in their life on hold. I have seen people leaving their jobs, families, significant others and moving all the way from Canada to Mumbai to work as actors and TV anchors. One guy at my gym has recently moved from Toronto after giving up his job as an aerospace engineer. Though he complains of how stressful life has become, he continues his endless search for stardom. Sleeping on run down mattresses and dreaming of stars is a way of life for many who pursue work in media.

Like everywhere else, here too there is good news and there is bad news. Fame and money are portions that make the good news. High levels of stress, uncertainty and the great effort that goes in to making oneself taste success formulate the bad news.

Not everyone is equipped to handle the stress and uncertainty that come with being an anchor. When you have pertinent work you can flaunt yourself wearing high heels and thinking no end of yourself. However, when you are looking for your next project, you can forget all about your hair, shoes and your last accomplishment as you run around in your gladiators from office to office trying to grab work.

If you expect too much you may be disappointed. Accept that your overall journey will not be a breeze. If you attempt to enter this zone, be prepared for a roller-coaster ride. Sometimes it may actually feel as unreal and as crazy as a circus, but then it will also bring you some joy in bits and pieces. This business requires a lot of investment and commitment. Sustaining is not easy and everyone is replaceable here. So before you plunge into this business, it is important that you understand the nature of this work and whether or not it suits your psyche.

2

The Nature And Types of Anchoring

Every business has a certain premise that it works around. Anchoring is no different, and it is not devoid of several advantages and disadvantages. While you look at TV or live event anchoring as a potential career option, one thing to keep in mind is that you be comfortable working on a freelance basis. No one gets to anchor a show full-time or round the clock. Even news anchors who read news every day have to be at their desks for several hours researching and writing news when they are not on camera. News reporting is a tough business and requires putting in odd hours while being in the middle of every possible crisis that your city encounters. While I worked with Sahara Mumbai, I came across reporters who led a rather difficult life, especially when they had to cover a story in the middle of rainstorms or political upheavals. Though news anchors, reporters and journalist's work full-time in news channels, those in entertainment anchoring do not have the option for full-time work, unless they become producers for their own shows within a given channel (which doesn't happen a lot). There are a very few lifestyle channels in the country and the few job opportunities available cannot accommodate thousands of aspiring anchors looking for work.

Most entertainment anchors thus work on a freelance basis. Out of all those who pick anchoring as their primary work, majority of them do it along with modeling, acting or both. There are also those who work full-time somewhere in the day and anchor a show or two in the evenings or weekends. They treat it as side business for extra money.

Anchoring usually is a freelance business and not meant for everyone. If you are at ease working inconsistently and not very often, then anchoring can be fun. However, if you like structure and rather work 9 to 5 every day, then you may feel uncomfortable working on and off.

If you do decide on being a freelance anchor then you must make a mental note of the time of year when major conferences and events take place. These times are crucial to capitalize on. Holiday seasons like Christmas and New Years are also good times for event companies. Those who specialize in weddings, profit during the wedding season.

However, if you work as a television anchor, there is no specific time in the year that you will be busy. TV contracts entirely depend on how many shows the channel approves in a given time span. Even if you work under contract with a channel or production house then too you only shoot two or three times a week, unless of course you are doing a daily show. Anchor based shows rarely take place every day, unless you opt for news anchoring. News anchoring is domain specific and requires knowledge of journalism along with a job in a news channel. If you are not a journalist with a job, you will most likely be anchoring on a freelance basis.

Usually anchoring on and off can prove to be a freelancer's delight and a structured person's nightmare.

There are several types of anchoring opportunities and before we plunge into the business of anchoring, we must be aware of the options available. There are different kinds of anchor based shows under the two main categories of Television and Live Events.

→ Event Anchoring covers all Live Events, such as
    › Conferences
    › Corporate Shows
    › Exhibitions
    › Product Launches
    › Brand Inaugurations
    › Award Ceremonies
    › Birthday Parties
    › Weddings and so on…
→ TV anchoring can either be live or pre-recorded.
    › News Anchoring – LIVE
→ Current Affairs News
→ Domain Specific Shows – Sports, Politics, Health, Astrology, etc.
    › Entertainment Anchoring
→ Music Shows

→ Film Entertainment Shows
→ Reality Shows
→ Travel & Lifestyle
→ Talk Shows
→ Game Shows
→ Infomercials – Selling products on TV

Not everyone gets the opportunity to explore all types of anchor based programs. Some anchors are involved only in LIVE events and are never seen on television. Then there are those who only anchor TV shows while staying miles away from LIVE events. There is yet another category of anchors that are able to do both TV and LIVE anchoring.

Whatever you choose to try out will depend on three things – your personal preference, your ability/expertise and the opportunity presented to you. You may be very good at being impromptu but may have a tough time memorizing long scripts or reading from a teleprompter. On the contrary you may find it easier to read from a teleprompter than to be spontaneous on stage. LIVE events and TV shows have many things in common yet are very different in nature. Hence, it is imperative to explore both these areas in detail to gain a clear understanding of what each requires from you and what it offers you in return.

3

The Character Of Television And Live Events

How is television anchoring similar or different from LIVE event anchoring? There is one common factor in Event and TV anchoring and that is your ability to speak well. Other than that, Television and LIVE events function quite differently.

Television anchoring is technical. TV shows have to be recorded in a studio or outdoors, depending upon the nature of the program. Whether it is LIVE news or a pre-recorded show, it requires a camera, a crew, lighting design, sound system, scripts and a teleprompter. On the non-technical side, it requires a make-up artist, hair dresser, stylist and several assistants who monitor the smooth flow of the shooting. Everyone has their own task and the anchors job is to simply show up on the sets on time, get ready, get acquainted with the script and follow directions.

Television anchoring has a set of requirements that you as an anchor must adhere to. First and foremost, you need to have a good portfolio. If you are photogenic, you will have a better chance to work in TV. You also have to look very good, speak really well, be ultra groomed, and in great shape (unless you own the channel or are related to someone who owns it). However if you are not blessed to own a network you need to work very hard on yourself. Television puts a lot of emphasis on personal grooming. After all, it is a visual medium and requires you to be visually appealing. With competition being very tough, you cannot afford to not look your best. On most niche programs, such as travel, lifestyle, and fashion, the entire focus is on the anchor, especially if the show is anchor dominated. If however, the show is reality based, such as dance, music, comedy or talk show, which includes judges, participants, and a LIVE audience, then the anchor acts as a facilitator rather than the star. Still the anchors need to be extremely presentable.

Whether you are on TV for a minute or for an hour, the same effort goes into getting you TV ready. Though you will be somewhat pampered on a TV set, television is tough business which requires you to be smart and have people skills. You will have people fussing all over you. In television, there are many people available to assist the anchor. Make-up artists, hair stylists, assistant directors, production crew, everyone will be at your service. Their focus will be on making you perfection personified.

Nothing goes unnoticed on television. Every hair, every piece of jewelry has to be perfectly placed. Even the slightest crease on your outfit will stimulate a discussion until it is properly ironed. If you want to be a TV anchor, it is advisable that you learn the art of patience. If you know how to deal with different people on all different levels, from the director to the spot boy, you will benefit. You must know how to manage communication effectively with everyone.

The good thing while anchoring a TV show which is being pre-recorded is that you can goof up. There are several takes that happen while shooting a show. Sometimes the anchor fumbles and at other times there are technical difficulties. You will have a chance for retakes and as a result you can better your performance.

On the other hand, a LIVE event does not give you an opportunity to turn back the clock. You only get one chance to deliver. LIVE event means that you do not get a second chance. A goof up cannot be corrected; it can only be covered up.

There is also a little lesser focus on your looks. You do not need to be photogenic. Most of the times, event companies do not even require your photographs. They are comfortable meeting you in person. Hence you have some leeway when it comes to Event Anchoring. Especially when you aspire to anchor corporate shows, you needn't worry about being too glamorous. You need to just be presentable and look corporate, so that you blend in with the crowd.

Event companies look for anchors that have some experience with LIVE anchoring. Those that will be able to manage a crowd are usually preferred. There is more focus on speech, style of delivery, correct pronunciation, an ability to ask the right interview questions to visitors and facilitate a discussion between speakers on stage. The key ingredient in a LIVE show is your ability to manage the audience.

Contrary to how it is on a TV set, at a LIVE show there are very few people who will fuss over you. In fact, to be more precise, no one will fuss over you. You will need to manage everything on your own. There will be no stylist and rarely will you get hair and makeup artists from the clients end. Either you hire your own artists or you do your makeup and hair yourself.

Once you reach the venue of the event, you will be so busy anchoring and interviewing that you will have no time to step away and take a second look at yourself. Event anchoring requires standing for long hours and being on your toes for as long as the event lasts. You will be expected to work efficiently and will not receive any form of pampering. So do not expect royal treatment at a LIVE event. If you carry with you a prince or princess syndrome, then working at events is not your domain, for they will not offer you a crown. They will make your feet soar and raise your temper high. They will push you in all directions and make you literally run around. Anchoring a LIVE event is a different ball game altogether and does not have much in common with television. Yet if you can manage it, more power to you.

There are several other differences between TV and Events. One of them is the element of fame. When you are on national television, your exposure is much wider. Anyone could be watching you in any city or town. However, an event offers you restricted exposure. Though the exposure may not be as wide, you still get a chance to meet your audience directly and are more likely to network with them. Whereas, while recording a TV show you only communicate to the camera and remain oblivious to who is watching you. Whether you decide to work in television or anchor events, it is entirely your prerogative.

Remember, if you want to be on TV you need to stand out from the crowd. If you want to be part of a LIVE corporate event, you need to blend in with the crowd.

Whatever path you decide to walk on, you may wish to consider getting knowledge about it. Let us explore if you should opt for formal training or are you better off being a natural.

4

Formal Training Versus Experiential Learning – Should You Attend Training Schools?

There is often a lot of emphasis on formal training in most cultures and some amount of training may help you polish your already existing skills. However, simply going to a training school will not turn you into a good anchor nor will it ensure that you will get work. This may sound like good news to many that anchoring does not require a certification or degree. This is one career path where your educational qualifications or the lack of won't bother anyone. People will assess you on the basis of your communication skills, your overall personality and your looks. Even if you are intellectually bankrupt no one will care as long as you are gifted with good communication skills and do not bug people you work with.

If you are a natural born speaker and have had some experience speaking in public, you may surpass going to a training institute. However, if you are completely raw and have had absolutely no experience speaking in front of people or the camera, you may consider enrolling into a short-term program. Most anchoring programs are short-term as it is not rocket science. The concepts are quite easy to grasp and most of it is practical. Anchoring is practical work. Similar to swimming where you have to jump into the water to learn, anchoring skills get strengthened only as you begin to speak in public. Though training can provide you some tips and enhance your knowledge, the process remains experiential. You have to do it to gain command on it.

When you understand the possibilities and limitations of formal training, you will be better equipped to decide whether you should enroll into a training program or not.

Firstly ask yourself a few key questions. Do I require training? If yes, where to seek training? Whom to seek training from and when to seek training? There may be plenty of institutes in your city to choose from. You must carefully select a school if you deeply desire to seek formal training. Beware of institutes that are fraudulent. Many institutes are money making agencies which may promise to make you a star anchor by the end of the course. They do not sell education, they sell promises. Do not buy into it or fall into their trap. They will take your money, put you into tiny dim classrooms, offer crappy lectures which even a dummy may find unintelligent and bid goodbye once your time is up there. They will waste your time, your money and your mind, all of which are precious.

Some institutes will guarantee placements to entice you but be extra careful of them. No one can guarantee work and no one can promise placements unless they have their own channel. There are institutes like that as well, who train anchors and place them in their own channel. These anchors get stuck working for the same channel associated with their institute. They get caught up in a short-term loop of limited exposure. They only get to host a show for that particular channel and easily get replaced by other students. Hence, their life span on television stays limited.

While researching institutes you must know who is training you? Has your trainer been an anchor? If not, then do not seek training at an institute where the desk boy/girl is teaching you how to anchor. Sometimes when the expert trainers quit, the office staff may be asked to step in to take a few lectures to save face. Many schools may boast of faculty members that you may not see once you enroll. Be aware of the current faculty and their qualifications. Only good trainers can offer you excellent tips that will help enhance your knowledge base. The quality of your trainer will depict the quality of your learning.

When you go to check out a prospective training institute talk to existing students. Ask them questions about their experience at the institute. You can even request to meet the faculty. If the faculty turns out disappointing, do not enroll.

If you are an International student, the schools might charge you more. Talk to the current students and enquire about the fee that the locals are paying. You do not want to get conned by an educational institute.

Sharmaine's Story

Sharmaine came down from Mauritius to enroll into a Radio Jockey program at a Media School in Mumbai. She was asked to pay ₹30,000 as fee for a one-month course. Jhanvi, the head of marketing at the institute offered her accommodation in her apartment for another 5,000 Rupees. After she paid up and attended the class, she realized that the course being offered was for Television Anchoring and had nothing to do with Radio. After speaking to other fellow students who were locals, she learned that they had paid ₹3,000 for the course where as she was paying 10 times more. The school refused to refund her money and coaxed her to complete the course. During that month, one fine day Jhanvi locked Sharmaine in the house and went out. This made the young student nervous and she revolted and moved out of the apartment. This further enraged Jhanvi and she refused to hand over the certification for the course to Sharmaine, once it was over. After getting mentally harassed for days, Sharmaine asked her uncle to intervene. Finally after a huge fight and a lot of negative drama, they got the certificate from the school. Disappointed by the experience, Sharmaine flew back to Mauritius with the certificate which came to no use and a bad taste of Media Schools in Mumbai.

Do not get enticed by the sweet-talking marketing person whose job is to sweet talk and sugar coat in order to sell the school to you. Initially, when you visit an institute as a prospective student the concerned person may smother you and offer you a cookie platter and later the same person may offer you a misery platter. Crooks will do a 360 degree turn around once their agenda is met. Pick authentic institutes that will offer you a genuine learning experience and won't harass you.

Research the institutes thoroughly before you make a decision. Do not get enticed by the website. The website may have a picture-perfect building with a beautiful view stolen from a travel website to create an effect but when you actually visit the place you may be horrified by the run down structure and unhealthy exteriors. Do not judge an institute by its website. Visit them, see the classrooms, take a tour, talk to students and then decide whether you wish to study there. If they put pressure on you to enroll now, put your thinking cap on and evaluate why they are being so forceful. If you do not get a good vibe from the place, put on your gym shoes and run. If they are genuine, they will let you take your time to think and get back to them. Also check if they have been around in this space for long. If the institute happens to be in a tiny apartment, it will be easy to wrap it up overnight. However if it is in a proper building and has been there for a long time, chances of it sustaining are much more.

If you are not comfortable taking a full-fledged course at an institute, don't fret. Instead of seeking direct training in anchoring you may also opt for voice lessons or a public speaking class. Small indirect efforts will brush up your skills as well.

Everyone does not require training nor is everyone trainable. Some people are natural at public speaking while others need formal training to learn the basics. Some may even be impossible to train and groom for anchoring for they may just not have it in them to do the job.

Understand your needs and then decide what to do. Education is knowledge and it doesn't hurt. However, make sure you learn the right stuff from the experts else you may have to spend a lot of time unlearning the wrongs. An institute can only offer you so much. Most of your learning will be on the job. When you actually get to anchor a show only then will you pick up the nuances of the job. Little tidbits that you will gather about the business while actually doing the work will be different from your experience while making a sample show reel at your school. On the field, work is much more demanding and real. Real work experience will have a different flavor to it which you will only get to taste once on the job. Whether formally trained or not, there are a few things that all good anchors have in common. In the following section, let's reveal the secrets of being a good anchor.

Part 2

The Art of Anchoring

Everyone cannot be an anchor, let alone being good at it. Some people suffer from major stage fright and would rather stay in the background than ever stepping on a platform which requires them to speak in front of large audiences. I had a friend in college who dropped out of a public speaking class that was mandatory for students because she could not deal with stage fright. I have seen speakers freeze and fumble in front of an audience. Can you handle hundred eye balls gazing at you constantly while you deliver a speech? If not, then perhaps another kind of work may suit you better.

Speaking in public is not easy and it requires that you enjoy speaking in front of people. To some, public speaking comes naturally. They are gifted orators and know what to say when. Then there are those who love attention but make a complete fool of themselves by being vulgar. Nobody enjoys these types. Then there are those who have a pleasing personality but are unable to deliver a speech. Only a select few really manage to shine when given a platform to speak on.

Strong anchoring skills are a culmination of preparation, confidence, excellent communication abilities, great command on language, an achievers attitude, effective networking, timeliness, professionalism and dependability, just to name a few. On the contrary, excessive nervousness, stage fright, failure to hold the audience attention, poor pronunciation, lack of confidence and an inability to manage the situation spontaneously are factors which can hold you back and infringe your success.

In this section we will explore the tools and skills you would require on your journey.

5

Presentation And Appearance

How do you present yourself to the world? Do you dress shabbily or stylishly? Do you love being hygienic at all times or are you more comfortable being messy? Do you receive compliments for the way your dress or do people refrain from commenting on your appearance?

Personal grooming or the lack of it will often make or break your appeal. Though it may seem shallow, you must understand the vital role physical appearance plays. Whether you stand in front of a television camera or a live audience, thousands of people watch you. The first thing anyone sees is your appearance. Imagine meeting someone for the first time. What is the first thing that you see when you meet someone new? Perhaps you see their posture or notice their face, hairstyle, body language, clothes, eyes or smile. All these things and many more constitute physical appearance. If you like what you see you may go a step further and communicate with them. If you do not like what you see, chances are that you will not bother to talk to them. Such shallowness is often seen in dating and it also takes a foothold in professions that require you to be in the public eye. So take a good hard look in the mirror and ask whether you are TV ready?

Why should the audience watch you? What makes you different from the crowd? Your appeal should be eye catching and your presence must be felt, only then the viewers will not change the channel on you. You have to be recallable. When you come on TV or stand on stage, the viewer should be hooked on to who they see and what they hear. Can you create that kind of charisma? Can you hold your audience by your presence? You are not on radio. You cannot afford to have ultra messy hair or wear tattered clothes and still enchant with your voice. You are being seen and heard by a lot of people henceforth you need to focus on three crucial areas – Audio, Visual and Kinesthetic. Audio comprises of all that you say and how you say it; Visual is how you look and behave. This includes your overall appearance, clothes, hair, makeup, shoes and your body language; Kinesthetic is how you make your viewers feel by your presence.

Both Television and Live Events are visual mediums which require an attractive visual charm. A lot of folks misjudge themselves while assessing their appearance. Some think that they are exceptionally good looking and don't require further grooming, while there are those that have a rather negative self-image.

First and foremost, understand that looks are genetically programmed. Accept yourself as you are and then see how you can improve naturally. Trying to be like someone else will lead to disappointment and that is not what we are aiming for here. Assess yourself objectively, see your strong points and then figure out which areas need improvement.

No one has to be born looking gorgeous or handsome in order to look good. Being beautiful and looking good are two different things. Beauty is rather subjective because it lies in the eyes of the beholder. Everyone has a different concept of beauty so save yourselves unnecessary grief and stop trying to fit into the mould of beauty created by humans.

Groom yourself instead, style well, and wear clothes that look good on you; get a haircut that suits your face; arch your eyebrows if you need to; workout to look fit; do some facial exercises everyday to get a chiseled look; and most importantly smile.

The idea is to enhance your strongest features and do mild corrections naturally. Be realistic about what can and cannot be changed naturally. Your height will stay as it is unless you are ten or fifteen and trying to be an anchor at that age. You know there is no point obsessing over your height now. Worrying about it won't make you taller but wearing high heels will. So discover simple ways to fix the issue and get over your height dilemma. If you are overweight, exercise and eat healthy to get in shape. If you have a long nose, you can easily correct that with makeup and shading. You needn't feel conscious because a little imperfection (whether real or perceived) is what makes you distinct. Don't get over obsessed with your looks because any kind of fixation will lead to trouble and mental disturbance. Remember the purpose of your body parts and revel in the fact that you have all of them functioning well. The job of your nose is to breathe and smell, not to make you look like a Greek God or Goddess. Do your ears hear well? If so, then how does it matter whether they are big or small? Your lips, your jaw line, or your looks for that matter cannot predict your success. They can get you a compliment or two (which soon will be forgotten), but they cannot change your destiny. There are hundreds of examples of people who are picture perfect yet have never gotten a break on TV. There are so many who have even gone under the knife to transform their nose, lips, cheek bones and even skin colour, but their success ratio has not changed. If success depended on the so-called perfect looks, all good looking people would be rich and successful and all those celebrities that go under the knife thinking that it will revive their dooming careers, would be on top of their game. Unfortunately, that is not how this mysterious world works. So without being nitpicky, just concentrate on your grooming. Enhancing and improving your appearance in natural ways, takes time and patience.

Grooming is simply about fine tuning what you already possess. You already have the raw material, now you just have to polish it. If you do not know where to begin, ask people close to you who can be objective of their opinion and advice on styling differently. Research what services are available. Seek expert advice. Surf the internet for fashion and style to understand the latest trends. Visit hairstylists and take their opinion on what would suit you best. Enroll yourself in a basic course on makeup if you can. Meet a few photographers and get their feedback on which areas need improvement. Make an appointment with the dentist to get your teeth polished. Consult a skin specialist if your skin isn't glowing. Go window shopping, try on different clothes, experiment with colours and styles you have stayed away from. Look at magazines and see what catches your eye. The first step is to gather knowledge and become aware of available options.

The worst thing you can do to jeopardize your success is to follow the herd. If you try to look like everyone else, dress like everyone else, you ought to lose your uniqueness. You need to utilize your individuality, not lose it in the crowd. Do something different if you want to captivate your audience. Know how to be subtle at the same time. Going over the top may make you stand out but it might get you criticism instead of applause. So learn the art of balance.

There are several fine examples of people who have mastered the art of grooming. Princess Diana and Jacqueline Kennedy became International style legends and are still remembered. Their clothes and makeup were impeccable and carefully chosen. There have been several other political figures and princesses in history but they did not make such an iconic mark on peoples' mind. Amongst men too there are several examples of those in the public eye.

Grooming is the first step you will have to take if you intend to get in and sustain in this business. You do not have to be super rich in order to become super stylish. This is your business and every business requires some investment. This may seem vain but spending on grooming, styling and looking great, is your initial investment for your business. If you open a new store, you will put a down payment on it, paint it, decorate it, light it and stock it up with the best merchandise. You may even hire experts and designers to create a look that would attract clients. Likewise, if anchoring is your business, you have to invest in yourself. When your work demands that you be in the public eye, you want to look as good as you can. People want to see someone extra-ordinary. They want to be impressed and charmed by who they see. If you can appear amazingly well turned out, half the battle is won.

What to wear – Your clothes!

For TV anchors there is good news. Usually the channel or production house hires a stylist who brings clothes for the shoot. Some shows get clothing stores to sponsor them. There are different options available for sourcing outfits for anchors. Usually the director will give a guideline to the stylist regarding the kind of clothes required for the show. You may or may not have a say in what they bring but at the end of the day please understand that the audience sees you in those clothes. If your outfit looks good you are appreciated and if it doesn't you are criticized. Unfortunately, you cannot put a disclaimer which says, "Sorry, I am usually very stylish but today's theme is circus and my stylist is responsible for my clown look. We apologize for straining your eyes with this visual disaster." You cannot tell the stylist what to bring, you cannot tell your director to put a disclaimer before the show starts, but you can certainly carry your own clothes with you in case of an emergency. If all else fails, you can wear your own attire and look half way decent. Don't let them dress you like a freak.

Many times the stylist might get clothes that do not fit you well, or are not vibrant enough for the program. To be on the safer side, it is best to always carry some nice outfits of your own that fit you well. Keep in mind the style and content of your show and accordingly carry something from your own closet. Shop if you need to, but have some stock in reserve.

Some channels do not have budgets to hire stylists. This could prove to be a blessing in disguise. Look at it in a positive way. If you have a free reign, you can create your own look (provided you know what you are doing). Most news channels that you might work for will expect you to buy your own clothes. Before you go on a shopping spree, get a sense of which colours are good for the camera. Ask your director or the lighting team in the studio. Most will suggest dark or bright colours for indoor shoots. Avoid white, pale and cream as they burn (not literally – it's a term). There are some reds that might bleed (again, not literally), or some colours that may jitter. You will have to be careful of which colours are safe. Get those! While anchoring a real estate show for Sahara, I would go shopping every week as I had to wear my own clothes. Though this can be a tad expensive, it's a fun exercise and its part of the job. You can buy a few basic things and then mix n match. You can play with accessories or scarves. Get creative, get experimental and get going.

For most events you have to usually have your own clothes. If it's a fashion show that you are asked to host, the designer might give you an outfit to wear. If it is a big fancy award ceremony, the company might hook you up with a designer to dress you in a lovely gown or they may ask you to get your own outfit. In the latter case, you should either know a good designer who will rent you an outfit for the evening or you should have something of your own. For an evening event, women should have at least one nice cocktail dress, a gown or a saree (if the event requires you to go ethnic). For men, a nice formal suit is good. For a day event, such as a conference, you will always wear your own clothes. So buy a stylish formal business suit. Conferences, exhibitions and corporate events require you to dress formally.

Your outfits are your tools, without which you cannot enter an event. If you think you can wear torn denims to a corporate event, you think wrongly. Clothes have to be selected depending on the context. Never dress out of context unless it's Halloween. Once I saw a fellow anchor wearing jeans and a t-shirt to a corporate event. She was bouncing around with the microphone in her hand asking random questions to visitors. Ten minutes later, she was asked to leave and I have never seen her again at another event. If you want to be taken seriously in your workplace then dress and work appropriately.

When I first moved to Mumbai and entered my first meeting with a well known model coordinator, the first feedback I received was to dress better. Since I was right out of college, I had a hangover of "the casual look". There was nothing stylish about my outfit – faded denims and a blue t-shirt that said Tommy Girl failed to impress this wise old man. Whenever he saw me, he constantly nagged me to dress differently especially when going for modeling and anchoring assignments. His advice was priceless because I soon realized that if you want the part, you have to dress the part.

Don't dress for what you were, dress for what you want to be.

You are not in college anymore; you are in the workplace where people make snap judgments. Show them that you know who you are and what you are capable of. The better you dress, the more confident you will be. Good dressing and good grooming enhance your self-confidence and self-image. So what are you waiting for? Go out there and experiment with your looks, and while you do that, have some fun.

Checklist of items to have for women

- A pair of comfortable formal shoes (black preferably)
- A formal business suit (smart blazers, trousers/skirts depending on your comfort level)
- A few nice shirts in different colours
- A gown (for an evening event)
- A formal stylish dress for a conference (optional)
- Pearls or stud earrings
- A stylish neck piece
- A light weight bracelet or a nice ring
- A watch

Additionally, women should carry with them a small makeup bag with their essential items like lipstick, compact, mascara, and eyeliner for occasional touch up.

A nice deodorant, lens solution and extra lenses, are a few other things to keep in your bag. Always carry your glasses if you wear them. Don't forget to carry other personal items that you may require. Once you reach the venue you will not have time to go back home and pick up things that you forgot. So pack wisely. Carry neutral shades of innerwear with you, else you may have wardrobe issues accompanied by moments of panic at the workplace. Your costume is your main prop. In the world of media there is extra emphasis on clothes. Hence, be careful while picking your clothes and packing them for a show. Depending on others for your stuff is a foolish proposition. So depend on your own self as much as possible. Carry your artificial jewelry but do not carry anything expensive with you. Use your discretion while deciding what to take to a show.

Checklist of items to have for men

- A formal business suit (Blazer, coat, trousers)
- A few nice shirts in different colours
- A tie
- Formal Shoes (black or brown depending upon the colour of the suit)
- A watch

Men have it slightly simpler in this arena, especially if they work in events. Guys who anchor events may not need makeup. On television however, they would be required to wear makeup. They needn't carry a kit as makeup is provided on the set for everyone. They can carry essential items like lenses, glasses, deodorant and cologne.

Beauty is skin deep – Taking care of your skin

Grooming is not only about clothes and makeup. There is a lot more involved. A good skin care routine is essential as well. Cleanse; tone; moisturize and use sun block regularly. Use a good eye cream which will reduce dark circles and puffiness. Always use products that suit your skin type. If you have oily skin, get products that are custom-made for oily skin. Don't use what your friend uses. Your friend may have dry or combination skin and you may end up getting a reaction after applying what he/she does. Before buying new products, test them on your skin. Get testers from stores and try before you buy. If you are acne-prone, consult a good skin specialist. Stay away from dust, drink plenty of water and stay hydrated. You are what you eat. If you eat French fries every day, your skin will resemble a fried potato. If you eat fresh fruits and vegetables, you are more likely to have smooth skin that glows. Choose foods that are skin friendly. Exercise releases toxins and makes the skin glow, so a jog on the beach will help tremendously. Lack of sleep, stress, alcohol and smoke are your skins' worst enemies. Stay away from them and enjoy being healthy.

Understand the role weather plays on your skin. Is the weather skin friendly in the city where you reside? Is the water harsh? Are the pollutants too many? Is it too hot? Though you do need sufficient sunlight for vitamin D, excessive sun exposure is harmful to the skin. Using a good sun block can help. Carrying a small umbrella is also a solution to avoid harsh sunrays. If the pollution is high in your city, then take extra care. Dust and pollution trigger the sinuses, so use a mask that will protect you. Wash your face once you return home from outside. Being slightly conscientious of these simple things will help a great deal. Following a basic skin care routine will ease your skin of external stressors.

You are what you eat - Food & Beverage

When and what do you eat? Do you eat balanced meals? Do you eat at regular intervals? Before you leave your house in the morning do you have a healthy breakfast? When you are on the go, do you stop and have lunch or carry a snack with you? Do you fuel your body during the day or you let it run tirelessly until you wind up and come home?

Food is essential to our survival, yet often times we pay no attention to when and what we eat. Being caught up in the rat race, in the middle of day to day chaos; we often forget that we work so much to fulfill this basic need – the need for food. Water and air are available for free but food has to be earned. Still we lose sight of this, don't pay too much attention to it and run after work, money, success and fame amongst other things.

The first thing to comprehend is that food is fuel for the body. Food is our friend, it is not the enemy. Being health conscious is fine but getting obsessed with being super skinny is dangerous. A lot of people who work in media are concerned with looking good. In the quest for looking good, feeling good takes a backseat. Swayed by false promises that fad diets offer, both men and women get caught in this web.

Though it is easy to get caught by diet fads, beware! There are a zillion books on diet and weight loss, there are also thousands of opinions floating around and there is no dearth of free advice. Whether it is your gym instructor or your friend, everyone has an opinion on what they think is best for you. Take advice very carefully with a grain of salt. Your gym instructor might be an expert on your workout but don't let them convince you on only having salads or boiled food. Your body will go in deprivation mode on a restricted diet. You may lose weight temporarily on a salad and protein diet but how long will you be able to sustain this diet?

I have come across so many guys at my gym who do not eat for an entire day before a photo shoot. One even goes to the extent of not drinking water for two days before a shoot. This kind of self-destruction has neither made him a star nor a supermodel; it has only made him nuts. Such madness is extremely harmful especially later on in life. Your body has immense power but when taken to extremes it weakens. Over experimenting with it and shocking it will damage your immune system. Do not take good health for granted. If you are blessed with good health, take care of it, maintain it and enjoy it for as long as you can. Don't push it in the wrong direction, else you may lose it. Along with your health you will also lose energy and your mind.

In order to keep your energy levels high, you need to incorporate the right foods. Eating on time and having nutritious foods will serve you. If you wish to keep your energy levels in optimal condition, eat well.

Not only the body but the mind too gets affected with when, what and how you eat. When I first moved to Mumbai and stepped into the dietician's apartment, she weighed me. I was a healthy and happy seventy kilos. My friends had begun referring me as baby panda. Though it sound cute it was certainly not pleasant to hear. Seeing my weight on the scale the dietician too was not pleased and gave me a life membership. As she wrote a rather frugal meal plan and guaranteed weight loss, I looked around the beautiful apartment and interacted with fellow dieters. Some of the new members looked happy as they launched themselves into a weight loss plan, while the others looked famished having gone from being "Winnie the Pooh" to "Skinny the Pooh". When my diet plan was made, I was thrilled with the hope of shedding a few pounds in the coming months, so that I could make a portfolio and start meeting people for work. I was told by many that I needed to lose weight if I really wished to work as an anchor. Hearing that, I easily relented to change my diet. The celebrity dietician recommended that I eat a small banana for breakfast with a cup of tea; for lunch one khakra (extra-thin crispy slice of wheat) and boiled vegetables; in the evening, as a snack, I could have bhel (puffy rice you get on the streets of Mumbai) and for dinner some boiled lentils, wheat roti (bread) and salad. Wow! I thought to myself that this was the cheapest and easiest meal plan I ever came across. Actually this was the only meal plan that I had ever come across. I had never created a list of food items to be eaten. She strictly told me to have no oil or white salt and eat very less sugar. I wondered where the real food was in this plan. This was a starvation plan especially after what I was used to eating.

In the US, my diet was super rich in calories – pancakes and chocolate milk for breakfast; Chicken burger, salad and fries for lunch; cheese cake and coffee to beat the four o'clock slump while gossiping with my best friend in the café; and for dinner usually chicken or turkey, which ever the cafeteria served. Then to keep me company, while I studied, there were the quintessential potato chips and chocolate-chip cookies. To add to the food fest, one of my floormates, Kristen baked brownies every week and generously distributed them. The entire floor would bond over brownies and then dance to the Macarena. That was the only form of exercise we indulged in. Since supper was early around seven in the evening, hunger pangs kicked in around midnight. That is when I would visit my dear friends Ben & Jerry in the refrigerator. On weekends, we had to do justice to living in Chicago. So we'd drive over for the famous Chicago style deep dish pizza, memories of which still make me smile, just like the brush of first love. I was in the land of food, wine and dessert. Every weekend, some senior student would sneak in beer and wine and we'd happily party. Each Saturday afternoon was reserved for the Chinese buffet at Red Dragon close to campus. Too much food and too little exercise made me a chubby girl.

Then to read the dietitians meal plan came as a rude shock for my body and for my mind. However, since I was clear about changing my lifestyle, I followed her advice. I woke up early every morning and walked for forty-five minutes on Sea face. I ate as she asked me to; though there were days I gave in to temptation and had the so-called forbidden foods, and of course I lost almost 10 kilos in a span of six months (anyone would with such a drastic change in diet and activity). Then gradually I lost another four to five kilos. After which, a friend advised me to join a gym and start weight training to tone up. Once I began working out, I came across gym instructors, members, models and actors who each had their own theory on weight loss and fitness. Some suggested that going on a sprout diet for a day would be good while others swore by liquid diets for detoxification. There were way too many impractical diet plans floating in the gym and none were feasible in the long haul. Under peer guidance, I tried a few things only to later obsess over foods that were not allowed.

Though I continued consulting my dietician to revise my diet plan and incorporate foods that would elevate my state of fatigue, it did not help much. The dietician passed away a few years ago and with that ended my life membership with her. The models and actors whose advice I had taken have disappeared from the screen and the gym instructors are floating around from gym to gym still giving random advice to their members.

I and many others like me have had to deal with low immunity, wrecked up digestion and fatigue. When you choose to eat poorly, deprive yourself of high nutrition, cut too many calories and obsess about your weight, you risk losing your health. When you prolong a restricted diet, you will definitely lose weight; however, a few years or even months later, you will also lose your senses. The body will react and you will see this in some form or another. You may experience fatigue, hair loss and weakness; your immunity may weaken; your metabolism might drop; your happiness might fade and anxiety may kick in. When the immune system weakens, the body gets easily prone to allergies. The repercussion of restrictive diets is not pleasant in the long run. You may look a lot slender, receive compliments and enjoy a temporary high, but the aftermath of excessive dieting is distasteful. Understand the side effects of restricting calories. You want to be fit and healthy but don't go overboard. If you ignore the side effects of a restricted diet - Hair loss, anemia, fatigue, indigestion, constipation, just to name a few, you will end up spending more time repairing your health than you will spend anchoring shows. Any kind of extreme is not cool. Eating too much or too little can both become dangerous. Balance is crucial. Health is a pre-requisite to anything. If you cannot stand for hours and run around, then what good is your skinniness? Being fit and healthy should be your primary concern.

Diet also affects the mind and the mood. That is why there is so much stress on eating well. Often gym goers and dieters restrict carbohydrates in the evenings, but they fail to restrict alcohol at nightclubs. Some brag about their strict work-out regimes and then are seen smoking non-stop outside the gym. One healthy habit does not justify two unhealthy habits. So make sure you are not fooling yourself.

Doing things with partial knowledge is also dangerous. There are several examples where people make erroneous choices. A lot of people stay away from healthy fruits but freely gorge on high density pizzas and burgers that do not have much nutritional value. Fruits are super foods rich in vitamins; they help elevate your mood. They have tremendous health benefits so instead of having a packaged health bar that you get from the self-proclaimed health store, peel a banana. That will make you healthier and much happier.

In the quest to lose weight, some people completely cut out fats from their diets. Understand that cutting out fats from your diet won't get rid of fat in your body. Fats are essential and the body needs fat in little amounts. An over dose of anything is not good. The body needs everything in balance – carbohydrate, fat, protein, enzymes, minerals, vitamins. Energy comes from food and if you go hungry for too long you will lose your energy, feel lethargic and disenchanted. Also, when you deny yourself of certain food groups, you will become obsessed with it. If you want to be able to exercise and run around, then eat well.

Seek advice but be careful. Eat the foods that suit you. You know your body best. Listen to your hunger pangs and feed the body when it is hungry. Drink when you are thirsty and sleep when you feel drowsy – it is as simple as that. This is not rocket-science, it's a simple process made too complicated.

Exercise

When you work as an anchor your fitness levels should be at their peak. By fitness I do not mean weight. Fitness means how healthy and strong your body is; your ability to run around and do different things; your enthusiasm and mental wellness. All of these things matter and make you fit. You must know your body's capacity and be willing to increase it through essential exercises.

If you wish to work as an anchor, you should be able to stand for long hours. Women often have to anchor shows in high heels, especially if the shoe will be visible on camera. While I worked in Budapest as a TV anchor, I would usually shoot three or four game based shows in a day. The shoes could be seen in the frame and the director would insist on having stylish high heeled footwear during the recording. Standing for four hours in high heels and talking non-stop was a tiresome ordeal. My co-host on the show was a guy who got to wear flat shoes and sit on a chair. Wonder why? You may not be able to comprehend why they make things difficult but you need to be able to take on the challenge and deliver the goods.

In Kashmir, while anchoring a travel show, the entire crew would be out of the hotel at 6 AM and we would go on documenting until sunset. I was made to sledge, boat ride, rock climb, and stand on a cliff just because the view looked great on camera from that angle. I had to even ride a horse on a hilly terrain while speaking my lines perfectly and pretending that this was the most joyful thing I had done. It was a rather difficult day as the horse was camera shy and wasn't taking direction well. Both, the horse and I, had our individual reservations and were not happy, as it was freezing cold. After several retakes we wound up and I got off the horse. Good ridden, since then I have never ridden a horse.

Kashmir is one of the most beautiful places in the world and yet that was one of the most challenging shows I have anchored. Travel shows require a lot of physical endurance. In Kashmir, we shot at all possible locations to make the final show look really good. We did every activity possible while we froze. I'm just glad they didn't have me swim in the lake. That show required a lot of stamina as the level of activity and risk were very high. Thanks to the gym, I was able to partake in all the adventure. When you host a travel show, you need the highest levels of fitness. Travel shows happen outdoors in the midst of nature and are usually shot throughout the day. There are only a few short breaks but mostly you are on your feet all day, smiling and talking. Be prepared and ask yourself a few questions.

Do you tire easily?

Do you have enough energy to stand for long hours and talk?

Do you feel enthusiastic throughout the day?

Are you adventurous and enjoy new activities?

Can you work well under pressure?

If asked to climb, hike, dive, bike ride, horse ride, parasail, would you be comfortable?

You never know what opportunity comes your way. If you are not totally fearless, you will not be able to anchor travel or adventure shows. If you have never indulged in adventure sports, you needn't be concerned. Exercise is a sure shot way to elevate your fitness levels and prepare you. Everyone does not anchor all kinds of programs. However, being ready for different kinds of shows, makes you well rounded.

If you have been a couch potato, now would be a good time to move from your living room to your local gym. Incorporating an enjoyable exercise routine, whether it is dance, yoga, kick boxing, weight training or just a walk, will benefit you. Exercise has several benefits. Most importantly it keeps you healthy, shapes the body and elevates the mood. For both your physical and mental toning, it is a one stop shop.

Take a few trial classes first. Try Pilates, Swimming or Salsa, if gym seems too mundane. Identify what suits you best and then take it up. Remember, being an anchor is not only about running your mouth in front of a mike, it requires running your body and mind equally well.

Crowning glory – Your hair

Your hair is your crowning glory. Your hair frames your face and can make or break your entire look. So pay careful attention to the condition of your hair and your hairstyle. What kind of hair do you have? Is it straight or curly; thick or scanty; long or short; glossy or dull? No matter what the current condition of your hair is, it can be improved. You can experiment with different styles and cuts which suit you best.

In the business of anchoring, you must be open to trying out various hairstyles. You cannot always stick to the same boring look. For your hair, you need an expert. You cannot and should not cut your own hair. This is a recipe for disaster.

When I first auditioned for 'Sitaron Ki Duniya,' a show at Zoom, I was sporting a cute bob. Though they really appreciated the way I spoke, the director was not too happy with short hair. He wanted someone with long tresses as the show required wearing Indian ethnic attire. I did not want to give up work over hair and I suggested that we use hair extensions. With great difficulty they got convinced.

Often times, directors have a mental image of the type of anchor they want to cast for a particular show. They look for that type and if you do not fit their mental image, they pass on to the next person in line. So either you understand their preference and create that look to fit their criteria or you forgo work. There are also those directors who have no concrete look planned for the anchor and select whomsoever they find appealing. In TV however, most of the times, the casting directors and coordinators are given a brief about the kind of look an anchor should have for their upcoming show.

Work on different looks. By different, I do not mean bizarre. Purple hair will draw attention, but it may not get you work. Pink hair may look good in a rock concert, but in news it is taboo. So be conscientious of the context you are in and what you are aiming for.

Use wigs as and when required. When you get your portfolio done, it is always nice to have three to four different hairstyles. Wigs and extensions can be a blessing especially when you have short hair. For travel shows, news, corporate events, short hair styles or even shoulder length hair styles seem neat and well put together. However, for shows that require a more traditional look, long hair is preferred.

Your hair requires regular maintenance. Invest a bit of time and effort into keeping it healthy by getting it trimmed, going for an occasional hair spa, and getting it styled well. Use products that enhance the texture of your hair and make it shine. Have some fun with hair accessories but do not go overboard. You want a refined look, not a look that calls for a fine by the hair police. With so much available in the market there is absolutely no need to have a bad hair day. Good hair will not only make you look nice, it will also make you feel more confident.

Keep stress at bay

If you want to look and feel rejuvenated, you will have to cut down stress. Indulge in good sleep, incorporate a nice exercise regime, stay healthy, laugh easily and elevate your happiness levels. Devise your own method to do so. Since each human being is distinct and has unique tastes, figure out yours and develop it. Usually even simple things such as a session of yoga, a relaxing swim, or a foot massage, can lighten your spirits. Find activities that uplift your mood and enhance your levels of joy. Cultivate a healthy hobby. Get creative – paint, sing, play an instrument, dance or try a new sport. Listen to music; play with pets if you like them. Plant your garden if you have one. Gardening is a great stress buster as well. Join a gym. Exercise releases endorphins – the feel good hormone. A little walk around the block can revive you instantly.

Socialize! And when you do so, don't turn it into a serious therapy session by discussing all your issues, real or imaginary. Sharing lightens the load but use your discretion while doing so. You do not want to create unnecessary stress by complaining non-stop. No one wants to hear about your endless complaints. We all know people who bring us down by their constant nagging. Rather than enjoying pleasant conversation, they use meeting friends as an opportunity for free therapy. Refrain from turning into Mr. or Ms. Crabby. When you share your thoughts and exchange notes with others in a light manner, it feels good for both parties who are conversing. Consider socializing as a way of creating more good times.

Your state of mind will reflect in your behaviour. If you want to stay positive then you have to avoid the negative. These two states are mutually exclusive and cannot stay together. Do something unrelated to your work that helps you be childlike. Read inspirational books or watch comedies to lighten up. If you are a freelancer, you will need daily doses of inspiration. Stay motivated and stay positive.

The more time and care you put into making yourself better, the more attractive you will turn out to be. Remember, your aim is to be a TV host not a TV ghost who scares people away. If you are a frown freak, get used to smiling. You will be required to smile all the time while speaking in front of the camera, unless you are reading the news. News is hardly pleasant enough to inspire a smile for both the anchor and the audience. Entertainment based shows however will require you to show a lot of happiness. The audience wants to forget everything and get hypnotized by entertainment. They seek to get hooked. If you are innately unhappy it will not be easy for you to pretend otherwise. So might as well uplift yourself and stay in a good mood.

6

Communicating Well

Anchoring is a game of communication. There is not much room for fumble and fall. You have to move into it smoothly. Communication is the most crucial element for an anchor. The primary function of an anchors work boils down to mass communication – to be able to speak in front of large audiences. Though we all communicate, we all communicate differently. Hence effective communication is far from being easy. Communication has a step sister, popularly known as Miscommunication. If your audience misinterprets your message, you have failed to communicate effectively. Hence it is imperative to really get a hold on your communication skills.

Communication is not just about the words you use or what you say; it has a lot to do with your body language which reflects your state of mind. What to say, when to say and how to say something, are elements that good communicators keep in mind. We all know the power of good communicators. People with good communication skills command attention. They capture the audience easily and effortlessly. The bad news is that everyone does not have natural finesse to charm others. However, the good news is that certain skills can be developed with practice. As we look at how to fine tune our communication skills, let's integrate and focus our attention on enhancing those aspects that are absolutely essential in good presenters. In the following sections, we will take a sneak peek into the world of effective communication, both verbal and non-verbal.

Communication is incomplete without speaking of Body Language. What you communicate through words is verbal communication. Non-verbal communication is communication which happens through your Body Language – posture, gestures, facial expressions, etc. When you stand and speak in front of people, not only do they hear you, they also clearly see your posture and expressions.

Words do have their place in communication but so does body language. There are several books on the subject, which you could read in order to understand it better. Here in this section, we will discuss the essentials of a winning body language.

What kind of body language do you mostly portray? Do you smile often? Do you stand strong and confident? Do you make eye contact with the listeners/audience? Do you walk elegantly? Have you ever objectively assessed your body language? If not, then please look at your photographs, look at yourself in the mirror, and ask people around you whether they think your posture shows confidence, ease and a winning attitude.

You could be displaying a negative attitude through your body language. Do you slouch; cross your arms while speaking to others; frown endlessly and create stress; or give closed signals to people? If so, then you must work on changing your body language. Your body sends constant signals to others around you. A genuine smile shows that you are happy, while a fake one is easy to spot. You do not have to be an expert. You just need to pay a little attention to your own nonverbal communication. Though nonverbal communication is involuntary most times, which means it happens naturally, sub-consciously and without much of your knowledge, you can check yourself to make sure you are sending the right signals to people.

Remember, what you say, how you say it and your body language have to be in tandem with one another, else people will not believe you. For instance, at a show when you wish to welcome your audience, you might verbally say, "Good morning ladies and gentlemen, welcome to our product launch. We are very glad to have you here." If you say this in a stern voice, without a smile, do you think your audience will believe that you are really glad to have them at the show? When you introduce keynote speakers on the stage, and say that it is an honor to have them present, do you really mean it? Smile and eye contact are two strong tools that will help you win an audience. Make sure your facial expressions are relaxed and pleasant, unless you are reporting a disaster. If you are speaking of a fire that has ignited you do not want to show how happy you are, or else people will think of you as an insensitive person. Get the drift of what you are supposed to say and act accordingly. In simple words, mean what you say.

Understand the context & content

Before you get ready to speak, you must understand the context and the content. Where are you speaking? What are you speaking about? Are you speaking at a wedding? Is it a news piece that you are going to deliver in the evening slot for a channel? Would you be speaking at a conference? Will you be anchoring a lifestyle show on prime time? Are you anchoring a children's program? Your style, the pace of your speech, your sense of humor, your body language, will all be determined by the context you speak in. While working on a program for children, I used a lot of enthusiasm in my voice to deliver the lines. Usually for kids an upbeat voice would get their attention and work wonders, but in this case the director wanted a low-pitched mellow voice with a rather slow pace, since we were narrating bedtime stories. The idea was to get the kids snoozing not jumping with high energy. If you are asked to read a news bite related to a fire in the neighborhood, you cannot smile and show happiness as an anchor. You cannot howl and scream either. You have to show neutral emotion.

Once you understand the brief and get a drift of what is required, you need to tweak your style. If you are anchoring a corporate show, cracking a poor joke in an environment which requires you to be rather corporate might backfire on you. Being alert, careful and aware of your environment always works. Before you start speaking understand the context you are in. Be thoughtful of your environment, the context and keep in mind the content of your speech.

Prepare & Rehearse

Do not undermine the importance of preparation. Before you embark on a journey you must pack important things that will assist you in your journey. Think of all the items you would need to take with you. In case, you do not have a few required items you would get them from outside. Similarly when you set out to be a speaker you must prepare well. A painting cannot be completed without a brush and a few paints. Likewise, you cannot speak professionally without having gathered a few essential skills. If you have had no prior experience, take a public speaking class before hosting a show. This will give you added confidence. Practicing the lines once you have a script will also help.

There are several kinds of public speaking engagements, some of which require prepared speeches while others could be impromptu, where you will have to work without a script. The former is easier as you have a guideline to follow. The latter however is tricky, as you have to really know what to say, when to say it and how to say it. Your essential tools that will aid you are as follows:

Scripts & cue cards

The script is your anchor. The script will anchor you anchor well. Scripts contain the content of your speech. Whether it is a TV show or a LIVE event, you would usually have a script given to you. Most of the times, the channel or the event organizer will give you the script prior to the show. Sometimes you will get the script half an hour before the show. Do not panic. This is very normal and happens quite a bit. Some production houses are particular that you get the script well in advance.

During an event usually you can read out directly from the script handed over to you. However, some event organizers will rave and rant if they see sheets of paper in your hand. One such guy went on and on about an anchor being unprofessional because she did not care enough to create cue cards. They may insist that you make an effort to create cue cards and rehearse a day prior to the event. Though these kinds may not surface very often into the event world, they do exist. In that case, you will have to jot down things on a cue card. If they want more professionalism, then feel free to ask them to provide you a teleprompter. Since having a tele-prompter costs money, these highly perfectionists event organizers will bring down their standards of perfection and professionalism. They will insist that you read from cue cards. So go ahead and buy a pack of rather large cards, so that you can easily read.

When I started hosting a music based show for Lufthansa Airlines, the producer's assistant would email me the script a day prior to the shooting. I would go over the script, make grammatical changes as required and practice it a few times, so that on the day of the recording, I would not look blank on the sets. The script would be in English and Hindi. So I would deliver one entire link in English and then say the same link in Hindi, as it was a bilingual show. We had a teleprompter in place which made it easier as it did not require memorizing the lines.

Channels, production houses and event companies usually have in-house writers to take care of the scripts. However, do not be surprised if someone asks you to write a script on your own. For corporate events, I have often written my own script and then run it by the company heads to approve it. This requires research and good writing skills. Write only if you will be able to. If you are not comfortable writing, insist on being given a script.

Sometimes, on rare occasions, there will be no script. Do not be surprised or alarmed. I was offered work on a game show to be anchored in Budapest, Hungary. When I flew down to Budapest, I had no idea that the show was unscripted and impromptu. I had watched a few episodes online that they had aired earlier, but I did not have a clue that they were anchored without a teleprompter. A day after I reached, I was driven to the studio to meet the director. He was a young Hungarian guy who spoke English with a European accent. He briefed me and asked his assistants to make me view the shows done in the past. The concept of the show was to play different games with the audience and chatter endlessly while doing so. It really did not require a script, they insisted. However, since it was a one hour show, I was uncomfortable when I heard that I would not have anything to follow. What if I fumbled, I repeatedly thought. Previously I had never done anything like this – no script, no cue cards and no teleprompter. I was reluctant to do it and thought perhaps I should just sight see and explore Budapest for a few days, then fly back. However, the assistant directors assured that it would not be as bad as it seemed. I was hardly convinced. The first day of the shooting was very taxing. I wore high heels and spoke for an hour non-stop, trying to convince the audience to play. I made a few mistakes in the process, which I easily forgot about. There was high energy, high pressure and a lot of Hungarians saying stuff I did not understand. Nonetheless, once the first day was over, I got a hang of the show and we recorded almost 90 episodes thereafter. I know how difficult it is not to have a script, especially when you are not comfortable improvising. While doing theatre at the University I was not too great at improvisation. I always required a script hence this was a tough one for me.

When you meet the producer and director to discuss new work, ask them whether they will have a script. Also ask if the show will be available on a teleprompter. The teleprompter will be your best buddy at work; it will help you a great deal and save you the agony of memorizing a long script. Having said that, there will be many occasions, where you would have to memorize the script. A lot of people do not want to use the teleprompter to save little money. They would rather not save time but for sure they want to save money. In this case, convince them to hire a teleprompter, if you can. I was anchoring a documentary for children on scientific discoveries, and requested the director to get a teleprompter. He wasn't paying me some great amount of money and asked if I could still anchor it because it was for an institute. I agreed on the condition that they have a teleprompter. Since it was science, I did not want to sit for hours trying to memorize only to fumble. Remember, the directors hate fumble. They will pinpoint on every fumble. Some even like to discuss your mistakes in great detail rather than just re-shooting in that much time. This is when you just tell them that you will re-do it nicely and move on.

If you depend solely on the teleprompter, you may be in for a rude shock when it does not work. On my first day at Sahara TV, I went in at 8 in the morning to record 'Property and More,' their new show on real estate news. They had assured me that the script had been uploaded and the teleprompter was ready. As soon as I went inside to start anchoring the first episode, they announced that the teleprompter broke down. Since technology was taking a day off from work, I thought now what? The entire script was in high-end Hindi and contained words which I had never heard before. We were allotted the studio only for half an hour before the morning news anchor kicked us out. So the show supervisor suggested that I quickly memorize the lines, in parts of course, so that we can get it over with. With his help, we got done with it but I was so dependent on the teleprompter that it made me anxious to memorize the lines. Such things happen however and if you suffer from bad memory, do something to brush it up. I took a two-day class to learn techniques to memorize lengthy texts since it was not easy for me to learn lines. You too can identify your areas of improvement and take up avenues to improve.

Your technical assistants

The Teleprompter, as discussed in the above section and the Microphone are your technical friends that will assist you to anchor well. They will make life smoother for you, so learn to work with them. Some anchors are afraid of the teleprompter because they have trouble reading and emoting at the same time. With continuous practice this fear will vanish and soon you will become comfortable using the prompter.

As an anchor or a speaker you will definitely need to get at ease using microphones. Microphone checks need to happen before you start anchoring the show. Usually the audio engineers will tweak the sound depending upon the requirement. You too need to understand how you sound and accordingly get changes made to the bass, volume, etc.

If you are anchoring a LIVE show you will need to pay extra attention to the sound quality. Does your voice squeak? If it does, you need to get the sound fixed or else the audience will get tortured. Sound is of utmost importance. Learn where to stand in lieu of the microphone. Standing too close to it will make you too loud. Do not start shouting either seeing a large audience. The purpose of the microphone is to carry your voice all over the place, so you can speak at a normal volume. The best way to learn how to accurately use a microphone is to make a friend sit in the audience's chair and give you feedback on how you sound. You can also ask someone who is a professional speaker to show you how much distance is to be maintained from the microphone. You will most often use a hand held microphone while anchoring LIVE corporate events. You may have a podium microphone as well.

While anchoring television shows you will use a lapel microphone. This will be very tiny and attached to your collar. You may have seen news anchors wearing lapel microphones. Whichever microphone is given to you, you will eventually learn to use it. They will make life smoother for you and they are necessary components of anchoring.

Using your voice & brushing up your speech

Whether you speak with or without a microphone, what the audience hears is your voice. Everyone has a distinct voice quality which makes it easy to recognize them. When someone familiar gives you a shout out, you instantly recognize their voice even without seeing their face. This shows how prominent voices are. They are as prominent as faces. So do not underestimate the power of voice.

Before embarking on an anchors journey ask "How do I sound?" Record your voice and hear it. This simple exercise will help you recognize which areas need to be worked upon. Try to understand the quality and texture of your voice. Do you have a child-like voice or do you sound mature? Is it strong or tender? Do you have a sweet melodious voice or do you sound rather commanding?

However you sound is fine. There is no right or wrong way to sound. You have no control over the nature of your voice. This is a gift and you must learn to accept it. The timbre of your voice cannot be changed. Having said that, it is important to understand how you can modulate your voice.

You can work with volume, pace and style. You can speak softly or loudly by decreasing or increasing the volume; you can speak slowly or quickly depending upon the situation; and you can make your voice child-like, playful, naughty, serious or even seductive; you can do a lot with your voice.

What you say is the content. How you say it is the tone. You can vary your tone. Try this vocal exercise:

Try saying this sentence in different moods:

- I love ice-cream (how would you sound saying this sentence if you were bored, excited, naughty, or upset).

How you speak will also depend on the context you speak in. If you are anchoring a music based show on television, you would want to speak in a light-hearted fashion, nothing too serious. However, if you are hosting a conference, it would not be appropriate for you to use a child-like or squeaky voice.

While working as a Voice Instructor with Kingfisher airlines, I would practice announcements with the flight attendants. When one trainee read the announcement, others listened intently with their eyes closed. They then interpreted the tone, voice quality, speed and other vocal elements to identify whether the trainee sound appropriate. You may have noticed how cabin crew makes announcements on a flight. A lot of times they seem hurried, they mispronounce often, they lack clarity and so on. Once on a flight to Paris, the otherwise very capable flight attendant announced landing at Charles De Gaulle International airport. Instead of pronouncing it the way the French do, she mispronounced it as Charles Dagollee, in true Punjabi style, only to create a momentary panic amongst the French passengers who wondered where they were landing. When you are anchoring a show, whether LIVE or RECORDED, make sure you check the pronunciation of words that you are unsure of. Freely ask the director and verify the correct way to say something before you say it. If you mispronounce, the audience will blame you, not your director. If you do not trust that the director or the writer knows how to pronounce correctly, check online. There are several websites that aid in word pronunciation. There will also be times when you say something in American English, but they will ask you to pronounce the way British do. Go with what they say. There is a man who makes educational videos for children. Though education is his business, he is the king of mispronunciation. To be politically correct, let's call him Mr. Pronunciation. After the anchors have recorded the lengthy texts, he will come into the studio and confidently proclaim that their pronunciation is wrong. Then he will insist that they re-record certain words the way he says it. You definitely do not want to hear him speak. Even on insistence, Mr. P does not care to verify the correct pronunciation online. If you ever come across such weirdo's, run if you can. Other than that, I do not have any advice. If you are okay with speaking poorly, you can continue with their idiosyncrasy. However, if you are quality conscious, then by all means, run away.

You want to ensure right pronunciation, clarity of speech and a pace which is appropriate for the setting you are in. You want to ensure that each word you say registers properly in the mind of the listener. That kind of clarity is required for public speaking. If your audience fails to get the message you are sending, you have failed in your communication. If after you have spoken, people turn to each other to ask what you just said, then again you have not been able to succeed as a communicator.

Be aware of your regional accent if you have one and try to neutralize it. A heavy accent can make you stand out but it can also hamper your success if it's not appealing. Listeners should enjoy what they hear. If you sound as beautiful as a piece of soothing music, people will stay tuned in. If you sound as annoying as noise, they will shut off the television or get irritated and change the channel.

Develop your speech and language skills. Polish yourself. Language skills are essential. Words are the verbal content. They help draw attention to your message. They help you communicate meaning. Often times you will be asked how many languages you speak fluently. In India, Hindi and English work the most in TV and Events. Unless you are working for a regional channel, you needn't worry. At times you will receive calls for shows in regional languages as well. So knowing a few languages certainly helps. The more languages you know the better. The more accents you understand, the better. The more exposure you have communicating with people from diverse parts of the globe, the better. Everyone is not a linguist, but taking interest in the language you are required to speak in helps. Even if you speak just one language, speak it well. Your vocabulary bank should be filled with several interesting words. Snap out of the habit of saying the same word over and over. If you see one word repeating in the script, suggest using a synonym instead of repeating it. The more redundant you are the less interesting you sound. Repetition has a place sometimes, especially if you are trying to ride a point across. However, too much of the same thing makes it seem monotonous. So give your script different flavours by putting in different words. Reading is a sure shot way to strengthen your vocabulary.

Fluency is a great part of your speech. Do you fumble while speaking? Do you leave a sentence halfway? There is nothing more annoying to the listener than someone not being able to finish a simple sentence. If you fall into this trap, do not fret. There is an easy way out. Frame the sentence in your mind first and then speak. When you speak fluently, you are seen as more credible, confident and on top of your game.

Pace is the speed at which you speak. Some people speak very fast while others are so slow they make the listener fall asleep. They are good candidates for anchoring bedtime stories. Understand your pace. Pace can be altered. If you are likely to speak super fast, slow down a bit. With a little practice, you can reach at a pace which works both for you and the listener.

Proper inflection and modulation are also very crucial. You must have heard people speak in a boring monotone fashion. Avoid being that bore. You want to entice the listener, not bore them or make them fall asleep. Give them some variation. Look at the text you are reading and experiment with how differently it can be said. One sentence can be said in a zillion different ways.

Introduce some style in your speech. Dress it up the way you dress yourself for a party. The more stylishly you speak the more fascinated will your listeners get.

Vocal exercise:

- Practice Saying, Aaa; Eee; Ae, O; Ooo, several times
- Practice singing to exercise your vocal cords
- Read long paragraphs out loud to become fluent at reading
- Tune into anchor based shows on TV and listen to how anchors speak (do not imitate)
- Record your voice now!

Record your voice while doing this exercise. Do you like what you hear? You must like your own voice and accept it as part of your personality. Do you speak from the gut or does your voice come from your throat? Initially you may not comprehend these technicalities but soon enough with practice you will get it. Listen to how other people speak. What catches your attention? What makes you annoyed? Listening often helps one learn. So listen from a different perspective and gauge why you like to listen to some people while you detest listening to others. Such analysis will give you a profound insight into what makes good speakers.

The Audience

Understand your audience. In all forms of mass communication, the audience is top priority. A displeased audience can be a cause for worry. Who is your audience? If you do not know, then ask the organizers of the show. Does your audience comprise of college students? If so, your way of speaking cannot be too formal. You might need to use some slang to relate to them. Instead of saying, "good evening ladies and gentlemen," you may want to say something more casual, for instance, "Hey, how are you doing? It's good to be here."

If your audience comprises of builders and architects, greeting them with a "what's up," will get you weird looks from the audience. Hence, it is necessary that you greet and speak according to your audience profile. When addressing builders, you must gather information about real estate and their work.

When you do a show where the niche audience is children, you may want to refrain from using complex words, or you'll lose their attention.

Be formal at corporate events and news based programming. At a real estate conference, I heard an anchor asking members of the audience how many siblings they had. She was being too casual and the audience did not respond at all. They could not fathom why she was asking such an irrelevant question. Could it get any weirder? Yes, she then went on to address a minister by another minister's name, despite him wearing a name tag. This surely got him miffed and she was asked to disappear. If you are naturally unaware of what to say, then perhaps a lot of training and rehearsal are required. Learn from these real life examples and do not make the same mistake. Gauge the audience. Some people respond well to humor while others may not share your sense of humor. Do a test first. Try something mild and see how the audience responds. If the audience responds well to you, then you have a green signal to keep going ahead with your wittiness. However, if you hear no sound, no applause, no laughs, it is your cue to stop. Learning to take the cue is important. You are not a comedian, you are an anchor. So let not anyone pressure you into stand-up comedy, especially if you are not comfortable with it.

Recently, I hosted a glass conference at an exhibition where we had a predominantly Chinese audience. Their communication style was very different from any other culture that I have been acquainted with. Watching them interact with the Indian event managers was interesting and hilarious. They were very direct, stern and did not smile. They did not make small talk with anyone either. While speaking with others they did not use touch. While the Indian event managers touched and tapped them often to get their attention, even when the Chinese seemed uncomfortable with this kind of communication. Totally oblivious to their displeasure, the Indian event managers continued tapping them on their back to get attention. Most members of the audience did not understand much English, so we did not try to use humor in our speech. Humor would have gone waste unless it was in Chinese. The moral of the story is, while dealing with a foreign audience, either speak their language or speak to the point. Trying hard to make jokes will only get you blank stares in return. You cannot change your audience, but you can alter your style to suit them.

7

Your Ticket To Enter The World Of Anchoring

Portfolio, profile & show reel

Once you decide to step into the world of Anchoring, you will require a portfolio. A portfolio comprises of your latest professionally clicked photographs and is essential for television. However, you do not require one for Events. In order to anchor Events, more than your pictures you need experience. Event anchors may or may not need to present a portfolio. Usually they would be asked to meet with event manager or the head of the company and get finalized for a show. In a few cases, you might be asked to mail your photographs to the organizer to show the client. So to be on the safer side, you should have a few professionally done up pictures, even if you intend to only anchor LIVE events.

If you aim to be on television, you must have a portfolio. There is no exception here. A portfolio is like a passport without which you will not be able to proceed further. Make sure your pictures have a few different looks. The portfolio is your initial investment. Meet different photographers, see their work, talk to them, and then decide which one suits you and your budget the most. Being comfortable with your chosen photographer is necessary in order for you to look relaxed and pleasant in front of the camera. Once you have shortlisted a photographer, notch up your personal grooming, workout regime and start gathering items required in your photo shoot. Your preparation will show in your pictures. This is the time you need to look your best. Usually your photographer along with the hair and makeup artists and dress designer will help you achieve diverse looks. You still want to take some time to plan your look and style. Once you set a date with the photographer, ensure that you get the right clothes, shoes and accessories. Usually all professional photographers work with specific hair and makeup artists and also a few designers. If you choose to hire clothes from a designer/stylist, meet with them and discuss the look, see their collection and only if you love their collection, go with the designer. Else meet another stylist. Do not entirely depend on the stylist to organize everything. You should carry your own shoes in your size and in different colours. Beige is a neutral colour and works with various outfits, for women. Nice stilettos, boots and sandals are essential. For men, smart shoes that go with their clothes work fine. As for clothes, for women, there are several looks, smart casuals including denims, shorts, skirts, dresses and/or ethnic wear. For men, t-shirt and jeans, a formal suit with a nice blazer, or a shirt with a nice pair of trousers works. The idea of having five or six dissimilar looks is to give a preview to the casting director of how you look in different clothes. Experiment as much as you can. Stretch yourself a little and try outfits before the day of your shoot.

You could be indoors or outdoors with your photographer. Usually photographers shoot your portfolio in both settings. However, discuss the location with them. Your hair and makeup artists will work on polishing your look and creating variation. Work with them without fuss. In case, you are unhappy with a certain hairstyle or lip colour, discuss with your photographer. Make sure your hair looks really good in the pictures. Hair can make or break a look. A good makeup artist will camouflage flaws, dark circles, freckles and highlight your features. Refrain from doing your own makeup. Just ensure that you get a good nights' sleep the day prior to the shoot, drink lots of water and feel happy. Your happiness will make you look fabulous.

Once you are done with your pictures, your first step is complete. When you collect your photographs from the photographers' studio, make sure they also give you a printed list of casting agencies, production houses and coordinators. Though this list will not be sufficient, it will help you get started. Contact the people on the list and mail them your latest pictures. Do not expect a miracle and do not get disheartened if you hear from no one. If your pictures strike a chord and register in someone's mind, you will receive a call. The call usually comes when there is a requirement. People will not just call you to chit chat. So have patience. Once your pictures begin to do the rounds and start floating around, you will get a call. Do not be surprised if coordinators flick your photograph from some channel or production house. This happens a lot. You may not even know who has seen your photograph and how quickly it can get transported from one end of the city to another. Let it be. Your job is to reach out to as many relevant people as possible, not to keep tabs on who has stolen your picture from whom.

Along with your pictures, you will be required to build a profile. A profile is similar to your resume, wherein you list all your professional accomplishments. Initially you may not have a work profile, but gradually you would want to build it up. Once you have anchored a few anchor based shows, events and videos, jot them down. People want to see your experience. They want to know that you have worked successfully before they bet on you. The profile you create will help you do so. Any achievement, big or small, should go on your profile. Make sure to include any skills that you have. Language skills; art; music; dance; cooking; driving; swimming; sports, etc. because that will help them understand you better. Having special skills also ensures that you could host shows related to them. Once I received a call to host a cooking show and it required the anchor to be able to cook while talking about food. Now I can talk about food all day but I can barely cook; I can only boil and fry, so I did not even attempt to send in my profile.

You cannot lie about these things. If someone calls you to audition for an auto show and you are required to drive, you must know how to. You can write anything on paper, but you must be able to prove that you are skilled. Anchoring is about practical skills, you cannot bluff your way through. So be honest. Sometimes people will cross-check to see whether you really did what you have written on paper. I met a director who was casting for an upcoming reality show. When I mentioned to him that I had been working on a show titled, 'Sitaron ki Duniya,' he immediately called up the channel in front of me to verify it. They told him that I was working with them, but I found his behaviour bizarre. Let me assure you one thing - you will see a lot of bizarre things in this line of work. Be prepared.

To prove that you have done work, you can create a show reel. A show reel is a video containing clips of your previous work. Channels and production houses will not give you the recordings themselves. You will have to ask them for it. Usually after the show has aired on TV, you can request the director or the assistant to give you a copy of the show. They may initially hesitate, but you can tell them that it is meant only for your personal library. Convince them and get a copy, even if it is a small clip it will be enough for your record. You can even put it up on you tube and send the link to prospective recruiters. Once you have a collection of shows that you have done in the past, create a proper show reel in a post production studio. Get an editor to make it look nice, beginning with your name, email ID and phone number. Your show reel will show the viewer the kind of work you have done, your style of delivery, your body language, facial expressions, and speech patterns. This will assist their vision. Despite having provided a show reel, people may ask you to audition. If this happens, go with the flow. Give them a copy of your show reel as well. Most of the time, you will not get work based on your show reel, but you may. So if you have it, flaunt it.

You could even create your own website, if you fancy to. This will not ensure work and is not necessary, but a few anchors like to have a website. If you have privacy concerns, it is best not to put too much information on the internet. You might attract unsolicited calls and emails, so refrain from it if privacy and peace are your primary concerns. You can get work without having a website.

Remember one thing, no matter how good your pictures, profile and show reel, you will be judged on your overall personality when you walk in. So make sure that you are at your best when you walk in to a channel or office to meet someone. If you look very different from your pictures, they will immediately point it out. If your profile says that you have anchored hundred events but you are unable to speak clearly in front of one person, they will catch it. These people are smart and you need to be on top of your game. If you claim to be someone experienced, it should reflect in your persona. Though your profile, pictures and show reel may help you, at the end of the day, you are your ultimate show reel.

So now that you have things in place, what happens next? Once you start making contact with people who are looking for anchors, you will be asked to mail your pictures to the channel, coordinator, casting director or the production house. After getting shortlisted, you will be called for an audition.

Audition

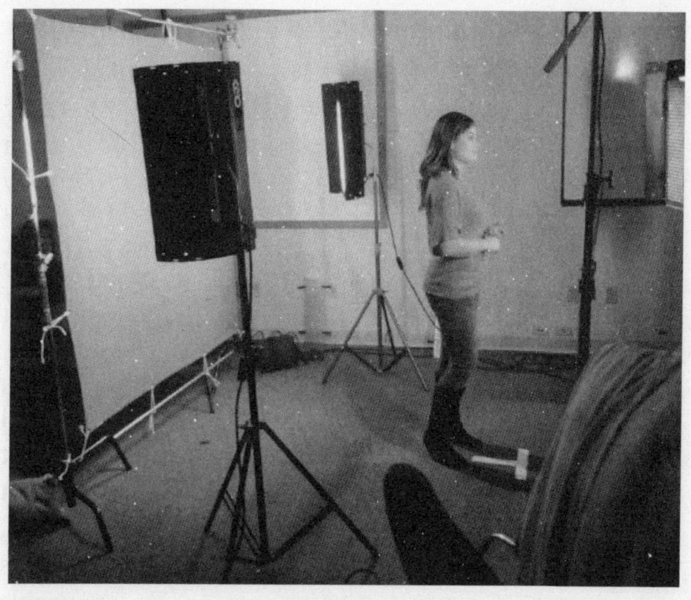

An audition is basically a screen test that any anchor must give. Once you are auditioned and shortlisted, you get a call from the casting director/channel/production house. A lot of folks do not like to audition. Perhaps it makes them anxious and reminds them of school exams. However, I have come across many people who enjoy giving auditions (or so they say). They use this opportunity to network, meet other people and stay in the loop.

Whether you like it or not, audition is a pre-requisite to anchoring a show. Usually after you have sent in your pictures to the casting director or coordinator, you get a call for audition. This is an important call and you must freely discuss a few things over the telephone before you get too excited and hang up. You will find that people do not wish to discuss anything over the phone and will expect you to meet them first. Even for small things that can be discussed over the phone, they will call you to their office. This is a huge drawback of the job because you have to get ready, look great, put on your best outfit, style your hair, commute for hours across the city, wait in the lobby to meet them, only to find out that they will schedule an audition another time. People who are calling you to their office do not care because they are not the ones travelling long distances in trains, buses, rickshaws or cars. You are making all the effort. So it is likely for you to get annoyed on a wasted trip. This is a common complaint amongst aspirants, that even to discuss frivolous matters they are asked to come to offices. Try discussing a few things over the phone to understand what you are going to meet them for. Many a times, nothing will come out of the meeting and you have to let it go. You must however get smarter with every experience.

When you receive an audition call, ask a few questions. Understand what the audition is for, ask about the budget (even if they do not disclose it, ask), get a clear sense about the kind of costume required. This will determine what you wear. A lot of times the coordinators will give you a vague brief. You may get a gnawing feel that they are speaking in code language. After being in the swing of things for a couple of months, you will learn to interpret their language. If they say, "we want a hot look," it usually means they want you to wear something western, something short and something that makes you look super hot. If they say formals, it usually translates into corporate attire, a business suit. If they say smart casual, then you could wear jeans and a nice top; a skirt; or a dress. If they specifically ask you to wear Indian clothes or carry them with you, please do so. They would often wish to know the length of your hair. Your hair style may have changed since you got your portfolio clicked. If your hair is different now, tell them so. Do not lie. They will eventually see you.

Once you are done asking about the clothes, check whether they will give you a script or would you have to give an impromptu audition? You may have to prepare a monologue and deliver. You must go prepared else you might get nervous pangs. Do not be alarmed if you are asked to audition in front of twenty other aspirants. Due to lack of space in the studios, you cannot expect to be the only one in the room. If you are lucky they may take one person at a time into the audition hall, while all others wait outside. This is not the norm however. So you need to get past your inhibitions. Initially you may have a few hiccups but eventually you will get used to having people watch you and smile. Pretend that no one else exists in the room except for you and the camera. This is difficult to do but try your best not to get affected by ten odd eyeballs on you.

Please refrain from getting into arguments with people at an audition. Occasionally aspirants go off at the casting director and at times they get into a conflict with others who are there to audition. Sometimes it may be required to give people a dose as they do act funny. However, try to be at peace. Casting directors and their assistants have a personality of their own. They can get evil at times, which triggers conflict. Some are partial to their friends and allow them to audition before they audition those who arrived early. This is a sure shot formula to elicit a reaction from others who have been waiting for hours and is enough to ignite a fight. No one likes trespassers and it is only normal to get annoyed. People who take auditions even get rude at times with the talent because they think that they have some power over them. A lot of talent will try and schmooze their way into auditions. Mind games do take place at an audition, but not always. There are times, when you will meet well behaved and somewhat organized casting directors as well. Do not be surprised however when you see chaos. Chaos is common at auditions.

The thing with auditions is that it is not an easy procedure. In cities where space is a major concern and the hot 'n humid weather makes you easily irritable, waiting in long lines for hours in cramped spaces can get bothersome. A lot of auditions take place in dingy little studios. Do not expect great hygiene, water or air conditioning. Once I caught infection from one such dingy place and coughed my way through the month. I felt horrible because I went to get work, not a cough. Be mindful at auditions. If you spot someone unwell, get out of the space. If you are unwell, do not venture into an audition; instead stay home and rest.

Whether or not you like the audition process, there is no way to escape it. There is something called audition etiquette. Once you have given the audition, send a message thanking the casting director. Do not constantly nag them, but politely let them know that you are grateful for the opportunity. Do not assume that just because the audition went really well, that you will get the work. Do not sit at home after one audition waiting to hear from them. Get dressed and go for other auditions. Gauge the situation to get a sense of whether work is genuinely happening or not. If your audition goes well and if they think you fit the requirement you will be called in to discuss the contracts, show details and the budget.

Part 3

Money Matters

8

The Art Of Negotiating In A Business Meeting

How you discuss money matters with prospective clients is a million dollar question. No business meeting is complete without this step. Whether you like it or not, you will have to discuss money. Nine out of ten times you will have to go through the negotiation process. Whether you work as a TV anchor or Event Compere, you will sit across the table and discuss remuneration with the client. At times this process will happen over the phone, especially if the company is located in a different city. You could also have a video conference. Whichever method you choose to communicate, the content will remain similar.

In usual circumstances, the negotiation process should take place in the clients' office. In case the company does not have an office, be careful. Though at times you may come across someone who works as a freelance event manager, in which case, he/she may meet you at a café to discuss the event. If the company's office happens to be inconveniently far, then too you could decide to meet the concerned person midway to discuss details of the work. This meeting may take place at a hotel lobby, local café or restaurant. Whatever the scene is, you want to stay alert while meeting people outside. Do not put your trust into someone new right away. The question you should be asking is when will you get the money and from whom? In a scenario, where you are not familiar with a company or its representative, it is best to clarify that you would want the payment on the day of the event, at the venue from the concerned person; else you may never see that cheque you worked so hard for. A few event companies offer advance payment to anchors once the deal is finalized. That is a good sign.

Clarify the method of payment. Will it be cash or cheque? Will the payment happen partially by cheque and partially by cash? Will TDS be deducted?

Also ask who will sign the cheque. If the person you are meeting quits the company tomorrow, who will release your payment? People quit jobs every day. Hence it is in your best interest to meet the owner of the event company to discuss money matters before you agree to do the show. The people hired by event companies will not be signing the cheques. So do not rely on them to pay you. You can be smart or be sorry. You decide!

When you step in to discuss the event or show that you are being considered for, the client will and should bring up the topic of money. If he/she doesn't, then at the end of the meeting, you should. Either they will disclose their budget or they would want to know how much you will charge them for anchoring their event. At this stage, it's imperative for you to be prepared to discuss money with the client and decide an amount which is mutually agreeable to both parties. This requires that you are prepared to negotiate. Most likely the client will offer you and try to settle on a lesser figure than what you might have in mind. So you need to quote a price which suits you best. Please note that asking an exorbitant amount will not ensure that you get it, so try to be realistic. If you have no clue, do bits of research before you go into discussing money. Study the market and get information from friends and colleagues as to what the current prices for anchoring an event are. Different events have different budgets. A full day conference may pay an anchor roughly Rs. 35,000* (less or more) and an award ceremony in the evening may offer more. The budgets depend on the client and whether the chosen compere fits in the budget. You may want to buy a BMW from hosting one event, but chances are that's an unrealistic expectation, unless it's torn apart structure is on sale at the local junkyard. Also understand where you are and how much is realistic for you at this point. If you are an amateur and it is your first event, then be grateful that the company is taking a risk and giving you a break. You have got to start somewhere, so prioritize exposure over money. If you are exceptionally good and confident in your work, quote a higher price and see how much the company is willing to offer. Those that have been in the business for a while know what to quote for themselves regardless of what the others are charging. Smart negotiation requires you to ask for a price that you think you might deserve and at the same time be able to come to a figure that is mutually comfortable for both parties. Rigidity in negotiation may create a rift. You want to stay assertive yet polite. At the end of the day these are the people you have to interact with in your business. Strike a balance and learn to assess when the client won't go any further in the negotiation process.

How to understand that the negotiation is over?

- **Understand the clients' body language** – This will be your greatest cue. Keenly observe the clients' body language, their gestures and facial expressions. When I went to meet the production head at Zoom, to discuss anchoring fee for Sitaron ki Duniya, initially the man happily chatted and seemed relaxed. Then when he heard my quote he suddenly crossed his arms, stopped smiling and began giving off closed body language signals. He quickly responded with a much lesser amount that he was comfortable with. When I convinced him to go a little higher on the budget, with great hesitation he went up a notch and then again crossed his arms. Beyond that point he did not feel comfortable to negotiate any further. That was my cue to stop convincing him and think whether I want to take up on his offer or leave it, because once he became closed off and defensive there was no getting past that. So try and gauge people's body language. The non-verbal signs speak louder than what words can communicate.

Listen carefully to verbal cues - People will continue negotiating till the time they can. Once they are done discussing the price, they will usually tell you directly or indirectly. Cue in to what they are saying. When someone says that they cannot go any higher on the price or that this is the best they can offer, you need to understand that dragging this further won't help. Some people will tell you directly that if you are unable to settle on their offer, then another anchor will be hired. These statements should be heard clearly enough and you should be able to understand that this is the final figure that the client will zero in on.

If the client won't budge after spending a considerable amount of time on discussing the budget you need to decide whether or not you are comfortable with the money offered to you. The budget should suit you as well and if you think it is too less and not worth your while, then you may want to reconsider. They want to know of your decision so that they can hire someone else if you don't agree on the price. If they want you badly, they will bring the price up to the extent where you too can be happy. In case you are not blown away by the offer, you can always ask for some time to think. Usually, in the real world people don't allot you much time and might want you to make a decision quickly. In this case scenario, they will put pressure on you to let them know right away. If this happens and you need some time to think ask for at least a few minutes. Step out of their space and make a call to seek advice if required or to think clearly of the offer made to you. Make a decision keeping in mind that if you say no now, will you lose business from this client in the future? Good decision making is crucial.

** Figures quoted above are for example purposes only. Prices vary depending upon the company, compere and the decade you are in.*

9

Contracts, Agreements And Billing The Companies

Contracts and agreements are usually pre-requisites to working with any company. As an anchor too, you will need to sign a contract with the channel or company you associate yourself with.

All TV channels will require you to sign a contract. Though they will expect you to sign lengthy contracts, the contracts will not be ready prior to you starting work. Unfortunately, it may even take more than a couple of months after you have started shooting for the contract to reach you. That is still alright but there is a mild glitch here. If you have not signed the contract, the channel will not release your payment. So you have been working; you haven't yet signed the contract because of someone else's inefficiency; and yet you are the one who does not get paid until the contract has been signed. So because of this, you suffer. In this case, request your producer or channel head to get your payment released anyway. Also pressurize them to get the contract ready as soon as possible.

Once you and the channel mutually agree to work together, you will be asked to sign a contract. This could be an exclusive or a non-exclusive contract depending upon the show and the channels policy.

Exclusive contracts

Most contracts are exclusive in nature. An exclusivity clause usually means that while you work with this particular channel, you cannot work elsewhere in a similar capacity. This clause restricts you to anchor programs only for the particular channel. The clause may have a few loop holes so read it carefully. The clause may state that you cannot work for other channels or event companies at all until your term of agreement expires with them. For instance, you are offered to anchor a music based show for the Music Channel and while you are on contract with them you get another offer to host a pet show on the Cat & Dog Channel; if you are on an exclusive contract with the Music Channel you will have to turn down other work. You may not be able to host the pet show. The Music Channel contract will hold you back and they have all the right to not let you take up other work. So be very clear before you sign exclusive contracts with anyone.

Some contracts are slightly more flexible and may state that you will not be allowed to work for similar shows on other channels but you can anchor LIVE events or shows that do not resemble the one you are currently hosting. For instance, you sign such a contract to host an Automobile show with the Auto Channel. A few months down the line, while your contract is still active, you get a call to do a similar show with another channel. Your current contract will not allow you to do so and you must forgo the offer. However, if you get a call to host a show on Real Estate, you could take it up because your contract allows you to host programs of dissimilar nature. You may still have to inform the Auto Channel of your other work so that your schedule does not clash and they too do not accuse you of taking new work without informing them.

Non-exclusive contracts

Prior to working on a show, clarify your stance. This should be discussed in your meeting with the producer and/or channel coordinator. If you cannot sign an exclusive contract, get that clause removed or altered before you sign. When zoom offered *Sitaron ki Duniya*, it was supposed to be aired on DD National and some other channel in Kashmir. So I requested them to remove exclusivity clause from the contract. My logic was that if the show airs on Zoom and the channel assures me a certain number of shows each week, I will gladly sign an exclusive contract, wherein I will not take up work on another channel with similar programming. However, with no guarantee on the number of shows to be recorded each week, I wanted to be able to do other work outside. The other thing was that there were two anchors for one show who would alternately host. So when the channel protects themselves so much all the time, why should the anchors not look out for themselves.

You will find that contracts are written keeping in mind the Channels interest, not the anchors. Hence you have to get the contract changed if you are not happy with it.

What might happen when you have a verbal deal with a channel and without seeing the contract you start working? There have been a few occasions when I have had to deal with the unexpected. When I was interviewed with Sahara, we agreed on a certain amount of remuneration every month. However, after working for two months, when I saw the contract and eventually my paycheque, it came with a fifty percent deduction. When I took this matter to the person concerned, he simply said that they would have given me the initially agreed amount had I done one show and some other unidentified research project for the company. I had no clue what research they needed to get done. Since I was only doing one show, they would pay me fifty percent of the agreed amount. That was alright with me since I had no intention of over-charging the company but I thought things should have been clarified from the beginning. Since the contract was handed over to us after two months of working with the company, we had no way of knowing what was really going on. All new anchors were on the edge wondering whether they would get paid. On the other hand, there was pressure from the show producers to continue shooting everyday and bank several episodes. So we could not even stop working until the contract was ready. We had to work despite having no paperwork in our hand. Eventually we got the contract and our pay cheque, so we considered ourselves rather fortunate.

Taxes

Usually if your bill amount is more than 20,000/- INR, your TDS will be deducted. If the company is paying you an amount lesser than Rs. 20,000/- they should not cut TDS. Often you will experience that people who pay you will take off TDS on amounts lesser than 20,000 and argue that they will give you work during the year which will eventually exceed 20,000. Try not to buy this story. These are usually false promises to save a few bucks at the time of payment. If you cannot convince them, jot down their names and number in your cell phone and put a reminder to ask them for a TDS certificate. You should get your certificates and file returns.

10

How To Retrieve Money When It Is Stuck

Recovering money after having completed your work can be a task that requires special skill. If the company you have worked for is highly efficient in clearing all payments, then you have nothing to worry. However, if the company does not care for your payment and fails to release it, you will need to follow up very diligently. In my experience, whenever I have worked with established companies with big names, the payments have come through smoothly. There have been instances though where the cheques have been stalled. One such instance that comes to mind is a recent one. Recently, I was under contract with Zoom for a show titled, 'Sitaron Ki Duniya,' when suddenly I had to travel abroad for a few weeks. Before booking my ticket, I called the company coordinator to communicate my upcoming travel plans. She asked me to send her an email regarding my plan and informed me verbally over the phone that it was okay for me to leave. The channel had hired two anchors for the same show so that if one travelled or was unwell, they would have back-up. Hence it was understood that while I was away, the other anchor would anchor the show and once I got back I would anchor. I had two months of payment pending with the channel at the time and I thought they would send the payment to me, like they always did, once it was processed. When I returned after about 18 days of travel, I was informed by the same coordinator that the management was slightly miffed by my absence. She asked me to come to the office and sign the contract (which should have been done before we began shooting for the show but the contract was not ready back then). We were in the third month of the shoot and upon visiting her I was told that the shoot had been stalled for sometime due to the delay in airing the shows. I signed the contract, met the director and clarified my stance. Things seemed fine and I was told that the previous payments have been put for processing. A couple days went by and I found out that the coordinator quit the job. I called the accounts manager to follow up for the payment. Initially he said it would take a week or so. After a week he said it would take some more time. After some more time passed by, he finally told me that the payment was on hold. I then called up the new coordinator who had been replaced by the old one. She gave her not-so-expert opinion on a situation she was unaware of and later informed me that chances are that I will not receive the payment. She totally warped my mind, so I decided not to communicate with her. I then made a few calls to the Production Head who did not answer any of my calls, nor did he return them. I sent him a message to communicate the issue and there was no reply from his side. After several failed attempts to reach him, I finally called up the director of my show. Thankfully he answered the call and patiently listened. He assured me that he would get back to me. After a few weeks, they came to a conclusion that they would pay me but they would cut twenty percent. I was not okay with that, so I again called the director to discuss the issue. He informed me that this was a decision taken by the higher management who herself was on maternity leave. I would have to wait for two months till she came back to work. They gave me two options – either to take what they were offering or to wait till the lady in question got back to work. I asked them to come to a different figure as I thought a twenty percent deduction plus TDS was a bit too much, especially since I was not at fault. Everyone travels or takes some time off from work. There was no logic behind not paying me after having worked for them. Again after a few discussions, they came up with cutting down fifteen percent from the total amount. This matter had gone on for over two months and I was tired of it. So I agreed but there was still a catch. They asked me to send them another bill with a new amount that they suggested. I refused to create a false bill for them and asked them to sort it out. To withhold fifteen percent was their decision, not mine. They needed to justify it to the company, not me. Finally they sent me an email that they would settle the payment on this new amount and finally the payment got processed.

At another instance, an event company withheld a portion of my payment. This happened because of Mr. Mood Swing, one of the partners in the company, who asked me to work full-time to market their upcoming event to get sponsors. I told him that this was something I had never done and would try it out first and only if I was comfortable with marketing would I take up the offer. Mr. Mood Swing agreed. After a week of meeting potential sponsors and keynote speakers with his event managers and him, I felt that marketing was not my thing. He kept on pushing the team to convince people to sponsor the event but the sponsors did not give him the kind of money he expected. That made him mad and he would take out his anger on the team. We worked relentlessly from morning till night running around meeting people without breaks. At the end of the week, at one of the meetings someone casually asked me what I did prior to this work and I mentioned that I worked as an anchor for events. That triggered Mr. Swing and he presumed that I was trying to get new work from the person who asked me what I did. He told me to not reveal to anyone that I worked as an anchor. Why would I lie? The sponsors would eventually see me anchoring the event so how did it matter if I was honest? Mr. Swing was quite insecure and got peeved with me. I decided that I could not deal with his mood swings and I quit. This gave him reason to not pay me. I did not care. I was simply happy to stay away from Mr. Swing and his endless moods. His moods were worse than a five year old. A few days later I got a call from his father who was much senior in the business. He wanted me to anchor his upcoming event. I agreed and after the event got over his father compensated additionally for the previous payment which Mr. Swing did not make. The moral of the story is that when companies want you to work with them in future, they will clear your payments. Else if they are miffed with you, they will not bother.

When you sense that your payment is not being released, do not delay the matter. Call the person who can help you get your payment. Do not speak to everyone in the company and start a vicious cycle of gossip. That will not help your case. Only when you speak to an individual who has the authority to get your payment released, will it help. You may have to make endless phone calls and follow up with the right people. You may have to visit the office and meet the concerned person directly. You may have to send a well drafted e-mail, which would also work as proof in your favour. Try to stay calm and do not lose your cool. If you argue with them, yell at them, chances are they will make the process harder.

No one can hold your payment, especially if it is a proper company. There are stake owners involved and large companies do not belong to one person often assigned as head of a department. Hence the producer, production head, programming head, etc. cannot decide that you will not get paid after having worked. One notice from the lawyer and they will have enough reason to fret. Though going legal is the last resort simply because it will be a long process and will require you to hire a lawyer, pay him/her and wait for long before you get justice. Being tactful and persistent will do the job much more easily.

Do not get scared of people working in Channels. They have absolutely no authority to withhold payments.

They may delay it, but they cannot hold it for long. The people who are in charge of production, direction, programming all have bosses they report to. They are answerable to someone above them so do not fall prey to their threats. They will make hundred excuses to not pay. They may also ask you to forgo parts of the payment because they do not want to give you the full amount. You may also hear that due to recession, they have no money left and that you should give them a discount. You will hear different versions of the same story. Do not buy into it.

To ensure that you do not get into such situations, before signing the contract, get to know the organizational structure of the company. Who is the highest authority that you will communicate with if ever you get into such a situation? Be very clear with how and when you will be remunerated. Be firm with people you work with. There is no need to be extra-sweet. Do not let them take you for a ride. Let them know that you mean business, even if it equals to not working with them again.

What happens when you work with individuals who do not run a big company and they run off with your payment? I anchored a promotional video for a renowned gym. The director of the show happened to be a famous villain from the 90's movies. The shooting of this video happened at the gym where we showcased its state-of-the-art equipment. After the shooting was done, the director who played villain in films decided to play villain in real life. When the crew asked him for their payment he told everyone to collect it from the production office.

A couple of days later I went to the production office to collect the payment. The girls that were in charge of the production told me that I would need to get the payment from the director. When I insisted that the director was not answering calls, they said he must be drunk. That gave me all the more reason not to try and reach out to him. I called up the coordinator who had got me this work. He said that he did not know anything about the payment and could not get it for me. Why was he charging me a percentage if he could not get this issue sorted, I thought? When I re-visited the office, the production girls informed me that the coordinator had already taken his cut from them. I was in for a rude surprise. That day I learned not to trust coordinators. They will save their back and not bother about you. After a lot of hassle and reluctance, I got the payment from the production office. I swore never to work with them again. Forgiving people and moving past a hurdle is fine, but only if the company plays a fair game. If they cheat you, stay miles away.

11

Dealing With Fraud, Setbacks, Unprofessionalism And Difficult People

This is my favourite chapter because it deals with the most difficult area of one's work. No one enjoys setbacks or difficult people. Not only in business, but also in life one has to deal with setbacks and challenges. Though they are unavoidable no matter how careful one is, it is necessary for everyone to be prepared to deal with them.

Difficult situations can have many faces. They can come in the form of your colleagues, event manager, or coordinator, a casting agent or strangers. Besides dealing with behavioural problems, you may have to deal with monetary or other kind of fraud as well. Not that you will always come across such situations, but if you do, you need to be equipped in dealing with them.

There is no fraud-proof method which one can apply at work or in life. Even if you decide not to do a thing and sit at home, you are not 100% protected from life's bizarre encounters. So it is best that you learn techniques to deal with professional obscurity. Every occupation comes with certain advantages and disadvantages. No vocation is devoid of shortcomings. So rather than avoiding work, you must learn to save yourself from boorish people. We are not mind readers and cannot predict whether the person interacting with us is honest or not. Having said that, learn to pick up cues. People send signals and cues all the time.

Watch out for time wasters. One fine Sunday, a guy named Moron who happened to know an event manager called me to set up a meeting with him regarding a so-called show. He said that it was important to meet this event guy the same evening at TGIF. Though I was in no mood to step out in the mad Sunday traffic, I went to meet them. When I reached TGIF, I saw Moron sitting alone sipping Bloody Mary. I asked him where the event manager was and he conveniently informed me that he was stuck in traffic but was on his way. So we had no choice but to wait. Moron seemed all happy and ordered himself a burger while narrating the story of his life, which did not interest me at all. He barely spoke of work. I was bored and wondered as to why he had called me in such urgency. Almost an hour went by and there was no sign of the event manager. I started getting edgy and asked him to call the guy. He made a fake phone call and informed me that the guy was going to be a no show. This made me mad and I understood that Moron was playing a game. There may have been no such event guy on the way. I couldn't do anything except to tell Moron off and leave. Later on I realized that he wanted to hang out with me. He was unsure whether I will come out to meet him if he invited me. So he used this tactic to enjoy some time with me. I was highly annoyed and refused to stay connected with him. The moral of the story is that people who are compulsive Morons will use certain points of yours against you. If you get lured easily, they will take you for a ride. So stop getting fascinated easily and stop slipping over false promises.

In order to do this you will need a sound and a strong mind. Only with a sharp mental framework, will you be able to avoid setback to an extent. If however, for some reason, you are unable to avoid hurdles completely, you will be able to at least deal with them.

There are cases when a company will finalize an anchor, discuss the remuneration and ask the anchor to block dates for the event. Then suddenly there will be no communication from their end. The anchor will not hear from them and will keep wondering if the event or show is still on. If this happens to you, call the person you had a meeting with to cross-check whether the event is still on. If they do not answer your call, which is quite likely, read between the lines. Perhaps the show is not happening or it is still happening, but they have replaced the anchor. Whatever the reason may be the point is that you are no longer doing the show. If the client acts unprofessional and fails to communicate with you clearly, you could blacklist him/her. If someone fools you once it is on them, if the same person fools you twice, it is on you. Do not entertain unprofessional behaviour and steer clear of such people. To fix the problem of getting dumped in the future, you can begin charging a token amount in advance to ensure that if there are any cancellations, you do not feel as if you have been taken for a ride. This is easier said than done. Many companies and individuals do not give advance payments to non-celebrity anchors.

No deal is final until the show actually takes place. Last minute cancellations are very disappointing and are lessons from which you must learn. The company will not reimburse you for your time or effort nor will they apologize. The business is hardcore and you need to toughen up. Sometimes your money will go and there is not a thing you can do about it once it is gone. All you can do is be careful as to who you give what to and why?

There are several casting agencies that place anchors, actors, models – basically all talent. These agencies usually charge a preliminary fee plus a percentage from your assignments. Before you pay anyone upfront, ensure that the agency is genuine. Visit their office, see the staff, get to know their clientele and then consider whether they will be able to help you. Even if they are genuine, their agenda is to sign up as many people as possible and make money. They are not social service agencies; they are talent placement companies whose agenda is to get good business.

Consider, how much are they charging? Is it affordable for you? Can they get you anchoring assignments? Check whether they only specialize in placing actors and models. Not a whole lot of agencies have many anchor based requirements. So before you put your money into someone's hands, think whether it will help you further your career.

Upon someone's recommendation, one of my friends and I went to meet a self-proclaimed talent agent. His office was located in a shady building and in the lobby were a few models waiting to meet him. We decided to wait in the lobby when one elderly gentleman from the neighbouring office came to inquire about the kind of commercial activity that was taking place in this particular office. On interacting further, we found out that the office space in that building premise was usually taken on a temporary basis by people. The elderly gentleman was slightly concerned with the workings of this man and he warned us to be careful. When our turn came to meet the talent manager, he boasted of having connections in channels. He then asked us to deposit five grand each in order for him to start sending us to auditions. I did not think it was a good idea to pay someone who did not even have a permanent office but my friend who accompanied me was totally convinced by this guy. That day we just had a chat and left. The next day, my friend went to meet him again and paid him two grand so that the man could start lining up auditions. That was the last day my friend saw that man and his two grand. That same week, the so-called talent manager vanished from the scene, switched off his cell phone and disappeared.

Another time I was duped by a man named John. One fine day, I got a directory containing numbers of casting agents and coordinators. I called several of them to check whether they assist anchors in getting auditions for TV shows. Most asked me to send them my profile but John asked to meet him. That same evening I met up with John. He had been managing work for a few known celebrities and spoke positively about his many connections in Media. He said that though I was new to this field, he would send me to auditions. He also mentioned how well people pay him to do their work. He quoted me an exorbitant amount of money which he would charge upfront. He also insisted on taking cash. Since I was starting out, and did not have any connections with TV or event companies, I paid him thinking that he will put me across relevant people. I assured him that once he lines up auditions and I get work, I will offer him 20 percent from my earnings. The moment I gave him money, he said he will start sending me for auditions. A few days went by and I heard nothing from John. When I called him he said that he was trying but there was nothing concrete. The man was soon nowhere to be found and I realized that he was a crook. That was an expensive lesson and John continues giving such lessons to new aspirants. I am sure by now he has received a PhD in Fraudulent Activities.

No one goes through this journey fraud-free. One of my event co-hosts is always asked for a discount from his client after the event has been completed. Despite having agreed on a certain amount prior to the show, the client insists on cutting 10 to 15% from him. Promising one thing and giving another is very common in businesses.

Important tips

Most cheatings happen over money. So how do you deal with this? The fewer the setbacks the smoother will be the ride. Difficult times or people do not come with a warning signal. They just drop in uninvited, sometimes even unanticipated. So how do we minimize setbacks in business?

Research the company/client before taking up their work

What is it that you should look into? Researching the company does not mean checking out their website or knowing how long they have been in the business. Such superficial knowledge of the event company, the channel or production house will not serve you. You have to get much smarter than that and gauge whether the company will pay you as per the mutually agreed amount. Most cheatings in business happen over money matters. So it's absolutely imperative to be very clear from the beginning over these matters. Hence, you should be asking questions that will enable you to become sure of the clients' you are about to work with.

Ponder upon these questions to gauge the clients' credibility:

- Is their office in a temporary space or has it been there for years?
- Will they cheat you in any way by not paying you once the work is done? Have they paid others who have worked with them in the past?
- What do other people who have previously worked with the concerned company say about them?
- Are they actually signing a contract with you or is it a verbal deal?
- Are they paying you some advance upon signing the contract?

- Is there a coordinator/third party involved between you and the company?
- Is the person who has recommended you to the company/client trustworthy?
- How and when will the payment be processed?

In huge cities, it is not easy to locate people who may change offices or disappear overnight. This is a very common phenomenon. Today there is a tiny event office where you go to discuss work and a week later when you re-visit that same place you discover a shady Chinese restaurant instead.

So how do you safeguard yourselves from being cheated? You have two options. Either you only work with big channels and popular production houses (which in no way guarantee a cheat-proof agreement), or you explore all available options both big and small that come your way and use good judgment. Realistically, no one is devoid of bad experiences and at some point or the other they get bitten by the realities of the city and the business. Although there are no 100% cheat-proof formulas to protect you, there are some very smart ways to outsmart the shady clients.

- Meet the client in their office, channel, production house or event company.
- Avoid meeting them in cafés and restaurants because you do not know how their office is or if they even have an office.
- Don't ever agree to meet them in their house (this is a professional meeting and should not happen in the house). Going to someone's house also means stepping in their domain, which can prove risky for

you. Whether you are a man or a woman, do not risk going to someone's home. Go to a neutral place the first time you meet someone new.

- Keep the meeting short and to the point.
- Pay attention to what they are saying. If the person talks about travel, coffee, their life, and other blah, blah, instead of the event or show, beware!
- If the client shows their interest in hiring you for sure yet hesitates to discuss budgets or payments, that's your cue to question whether this deal is genuine or not.

Do not try hard to close the deal. If they are not ready to do so, no matter how hard you try, it will be a futile effort. If they want to work with you, they will close the deal. If they do not commit to anything, it is your cue to wrap it up and leave.

How much should you charge and how much should they pay?

When I first moved to Mumbai and went for an anchoring audition at a health care channel I was told that they would pay me Rs. 1500 for an entire days shoot. I had heard anchors charging exorbitant amounts of money and here was this guy telling me that this was all they paid their anchors. Quite taken by surprise, as I was about to leave I saw a bunch of people rolling into the lobby and waiting to audition for this show. The production guy later told me that there were people who were ready to work for free. You cannot beat that, but I still turned down their offer. The point is that some channels and production houses expect people to agree to work for little or no money. Beware of this! Working for little money if you badly need it is still okay but working for free is a bit too much, unless you are a social worker. I have worked for free twice for friends but it hasn't done me any good. Professionally you should charge because when people have to pay they take you seriously.

There may be times when you discount your price for people you have a good rapport with. There may be instances when you'd rather not spell out your quote to the client especially if they give you consistent work and are on friendly terms with you. In such exceptional cases, it is okay to be flexible and rather have the client decide what they would be comfortable offering you. The head of Swarovski in India gave me my first event in Mumbai which I anchored for Bombay Jewelers at Hyatt. Since he was the first person to initiate me into Live Event Anchoring, I have never ever quoted him a price. Whenever he calls me for an event, I anchor it and he personally hands over a cheque to me thereafter. Whatever the amount is, I graciously accept. This is my way of showing gratitude. Nonetheless, this has always been the way I have done business with this particular company.

Anchor goof ups

There are always two sides to a coin. There is a famous saying, "It takes two to tango", which means that both parties are responsible for whatever goes on. One alone cannot be blamed for everything. So far we have been only focusing on what happens to anchors. Let's now look at what anchors do to goof up their act.

There is no such thing as a perfect anchor. Neither are they perfect nor are they flawless. They too make a lot of mistakes and sometimes a few blunders. Mistakes are fine, blunders are not. There are a few things that an anchor should never do. If you want to sustain in the business, these are the things you should watch out for.

Asking for more money after the show/event

A lot of anchors have a habit of settling on a certain amount of money during the negotiation process but once the show is complete and it is time to get money, they ask the client for more money than what was initially agreed upon. They go on nagging and demanding a few extra bucks to be added for reasons best known to them. This is highly unprofessional. Do not even think about using nagging as one of your distinctive features. Asking for more money than what you initially settled for is a sure shot way to put people off. They will quickly term you as a dishonest gold digger. They may also endow you with other names which will not be pleasant to hear. Once you have settled on an amount, stick to it. If you think it is too less, tell them so at the time of negotiation. After the show is done with, do not give people grief over money. This is a strict no-no.

Clients get upset when they are put on a spot like this. They also refuse to work with such anchors in future. They even ensure that all others get to know that you are bad news. Company heads who organize yearly corporate events and jewelry shows have often complained about this issue. They find it very annoying and never repeat an anchor that makes unreasonable demands for money after the show is complete. Anchors on the other hand think that these companies are like gold mines and a bit of nagging will get them to extract more. A few even go to the extent of playing damsel in distress. They make up stories and try to get more out of the client. Unless your intention is to make someone really angry and get them peeved by your behaviour, do not ask for more. Be grateful for what you are getting rather than complain that it is not enough. You were not put on gun point to do the show for the money you settled for. You consented to it, so be glad for it.

Stealing products/items from the event or show

How do you feel about theft? Some anchors enjoy stealing products they are anchoring for. They somehow believe that it is their right to take the product home. Just because you are anchoring for a product, it does not qualify as yours. After flicking the product from the show, they quietly vanish and the company begins to chase them. Any allegation makes the anchor feel as though they are the victim to false accusation.

Please realize that theft causes great agony to the client and makes a hole in their pocket. If you are given jewelry to be worn for an event, you need to return it. If you have been given a dress to be worn at the show, it needs to get back to the designer. Just because you have fallen in love with it, does not entitle you to keep it. Whatever is the property of the channel or company, it has to be returned to them.

The TV studio in Budapest had a well spread makeup lounge for all anchors to use. The lounge displayed all kinds of high end makeup products and of course to safeguard it from theft, several cameras were installed. A few anchors were too clever for the camera and knew how to outsmart it. They had learned ways to deceive the camera. Each week, things would get stolen and the makeup artists would make a huge issue since it was expensive stuff. The company had strict policy against theft, but kleptomaniacs did not care much for policy. They would flick and flee.

Avoid getting into any such scenario at all cost. Companies have a strict policy on theft of property. If you get caught you will not only lose face, you will also lose work. You may get fascinated by the lovely products you see but no matter how tempted you are, do not take things which do not belong to you.

If you happen to take something home intentionally or by mistake, have the courtesy to return it to the concerned party. No one will accuse you if you return their stuff. You could just tell them that you took it by mistake and later realized that it wasn't yours. Or if you are too ashamed to admit that you took something, return it anonymously. Whatever you do, return things that do not belong to you. Do not lose credibility. You are an anchor, not a thief. Do not make theft your side-business.

Not paying the coordinator their percentage

When you get work through someone who charges a fee for getting you business, it is your responsibility to pay them. Once you have gone thru a coordinator or casting director to meet a prospective client, if you get the show, you owe the coordinator a percentage from your remuneration.

This percentage depends on what you and the coordinator have mutually agreed upon. If the coordinator charges 20 percent of what is being given to you, you must pay that amount once you receive your payment. Failing to do so will create a rift between you and the coordinator while ensuring no future business from him/her.

The trouble starts when anchors try and outsmart their coordinator. They think, “Why should I pay this man/woman 20 percent? All he/she did was introduce me to the casting head at the channel. I have to work so hard and pay this coordinator just for a phone call.” Though this thought which has occurred in the anchors mind is valid to an extent, the coordinator has done his/her job, so they must get paid for it. You may think that their work is easy, but maybe it is not as easy as it seems. Give them the benefit of doubt along with their percentage.

Many anchors get to know of an audition through a coordinator but when asked how they got to know about it, they do not reveal the coordinators name. They prefer to say that they have come directly for the audition. If they get shortlisted for the show, they surpass the coordinator and get on with it. If the coordinator questions them, they lie. They are quick to say, “Oh, before I got your message, a friend of mine had already sent me for the same audition. If you have any other auditions, let me know.” Yeah right! The coordinators are too smart to buy such naiveté.

Do not burn bridges just to save a few bucks. Stinginess does not go a long way. Be generous and fair to people who work for you. If someone has sent you for an audition, admit it. Pay them their fee. If you think their charges are too much for you to be able to afford, tell them. Negotiate! They would want you to work because when you work, they earn. If you lose work, their cut also goes. So work on a percentage which is mutually agreeable.

Part 4

Getting Business and Staying in Business

Getting work is hard enough and sustaining is even harder. Contrary to popular belief, getting consistent work in Television and LIVE Events is not a small feat. There is a lot of competition and companies want to try out new people. They want to experiment with fresh faces. There are all kinds of people and ideologies in the business. Some prefer working with the same set of people because they wish to avoid trial and error. Their comfort level is higher with anchors who have worked with them in the past. Some companies do not care about repeating anchors. They may only care about the cost to the company and may want to hire those that will cost them the least amount of money while giving them a decent quality of work.

A lot of clientele will compromise on quality but they will refuse to compromise on the price. In a time of recession and cost cutting, getting business is an accomplishment. Every day hundreds of new people walk into TV auditions. Every day new profiles and photographs replace old ones. Every day there are new faces ready to be launched. In this kind of a scenario, sustaining is difficult. Though there is no guarantee that once you enter this business, you will keep getting work, there are definitely a few tricks of the trade which will help you.

We all know that there are many ways to achieve success. There are the straight forward ways and there are the manipulative ways. In this world, where everything goes, by making no mention of the obvious reasons how people get work, would make a biased viewpoint. So let us not kid ourselves. You could get something on merit or you could get it because of your connections. You could earn a position or inherit it.

If you happen to be the son/daughter of the channel head, then good for you. You will not need to read any book on how to get work in a channel. You will get entry into the world of television easily. You may or may not be successful but at least you get a shot at it. Getting entry itself is an accomplishment. What you do with the opportunity gifted to you will depend on your caliber.

If you happen to be the boyfriend/girlfriend of someone influential, then again you need not read this book. In fact, you could write your own book. If you make hay while the sun shines, you are a smart cookie. If hooking up with people to get work suits your psyche then more power to you.

However, everyone does not have the inclination to form a relationship with someone random just to get work. Neither is hooking up with insignificant others everyone's forte and nor does everyone have influential connections to help them move up the ladder. Nor does this kind of manipulation comes with a success warranty.

This section is meant for those who rely entirely on themselves and their destiny to make it happen. In the following section we will discuss a few ingredients that help people achieve success towards their dream.

12

Success Ingredients

Be excellent in your work

The one thing that will keep getting you work is your skill set. We have discussed this in the earlier section of this book. Do not undermine the importance of achieving excellence in your work. If you are good at what you do, people will hire you and re-hire you. People want to hire those that will do an excellent job. If they view you as mediocre they will look elsewhere. However, if they view you as the best candidate for the job you will keep getting work. So work on yourself and put your best foot forward.

The more refined you are the more confidence you will portray. People respond to confidence. If you are sure of the quality you can offer, others will feel assured as well.

Your level of confidence in what you bring forth has to be very high and that confidence will come from consistently doing good work. Make an effort to get better each day. Improve with every show, with every opportunity and with every project. Refine your skills and keep getting more efficient. There is no substitute to excellence. You will make it if you have the ability to deliver the goods. So do it and do it well. If you wish to become a high achiever you will have to get a grip on your work. Master the skills of your business and show the world that you are the best. If you believe in you, the world will believe in you.

Be recallable

After having met someone for work when you call them up, do they wonder who you are or they remember you easily? If people have a hard time recalling you, then there is work to do.

Understand that channels, coordinators, casting agencies and event companies get hundreds of pictures everyday and in order for them to remember you, you need to stand out. Standing out does not necessarily mean that you need to do something obnoxious or colour your hair red though such things will also do the job. Any kind of oddness will make you look different from the crowd however we are not here to create a circus. Our goal is to become easily recallable in a positive way. Standing apart from the crowd means adding some extra zing to your personality.

You need to become recallable in order for people to think of you when an appropriate opportunity arises. When someone is organizing an event or casting for a TV show, your name should pop up in their head. How do you leave that impression on someone's mind is something you need to think about. How you dress, how you behave and how you converse will all have an impact on the other party. If you are bland and boring, you have lost the game even before it begins. What qualities set you apart from the rest of the crowd? Is it your laugh, your interesting stories, your hair or your style? Is it something else about you that can catch attention?

Calling someone endlessly and stalking them will also make you recallable but in a scary way. The only show they will consider you for is a remake of host-turns-ghost. That is not what you want, so refrain from stalking someone. Your goal is not to scare people but to lure them. Identify something extra-ordinary in yourself and build on it. This could well be a personality trait such as your sense of humor or it could be a physical trait such as your sense of style. Figure out what it is that will strike a chord and develop that. If you want to become recallable in the minds of people you need to work on becoming a show stopper. Let the world turn around to look at you in delight. You have to create that aura in order to become recallable.

Network with the right people

Whether you are new in the city or you have lived there since childhood, you will have to make relevant connections with the right people who can assist you in getting work. Some people will be able to offer you work directly, especially if they own an event company or work for a TV channel. However, there will also be those who could recommend you to someone who is hiring. There are many people who are linked with channels or production houses in some capacity or another and can prove instrumental in setting up a work meeting for you. Only if you interact with people in social situations, will you get to know what others do and whether they can help.

People who happen to be in the same business as yourself would be the ones you will need to connect with. When you attend a get together or a social event do not hesitate to connect with people. Talking will only help you. So freely talk and listen. Let people know about yourself and your work. If they happen to be in the same business as you, they will speak about it. They may be hiring or might know someone who needs an anchor. You never know who you might come across and some people may help you get work. So be open to meeting new people and networking with them. A lot of work in TV and Events happens through word of mouth.

Exchange cards or phone numbers with people and send them a message a day later letting them know that you enjoyed meeting them. This sort of gesture is usually appreciated and helps build connections. Do not nag people however and refrain from bugging them by constantly calling them. Maintain dignity in your interactions.

Your job is to meet people, make connections, exchange numbers, stay in touch once in a while and widen your network. There is no harm in widening your network. Small talk at a party or the gym can go a long way sometimes. Be aware that not everyone you meet will be able to assist you with getting work. The lesser you expect from people, the better off you will be. If they help you get work be grateful and feel blessed. If they do not help you get work even when they can, be neutral towards them. Don't rack your brains over who has not done what. Stay away from all that negative jazz. If people are aware of what you do, they will keep you in mind for future opportunities related to your work as and when they arise.

Having said that, you also need to be aware of those that claim to own production houses and event companies, but in reality they are just trying to fool you. People who are out for the sole purpose of fraud have one intention. They want to use your vulnerability for their own benefit. They want to have fun at your expense. They cannot get you work, but if they promise you great things, they know you will get lured. Your great desire to achieve fame will spell out to them as your weakness. There are many men and women who use this hook to get a date with young, good looking and vulnerable aspirants.

Everyone comes across different people and instances. Your challenge is to be able to identify who is really genuine and who is trying to take you for a ride? You need to soon learn to differentiate between a genuine person and a fraud one. How would you know the difference? If you are not a mind reader, if you are not an astrologer and if you do not have a degree in social psychology, then how can you tell whom to trust? The answer to this is not so simple yet with practice and perhaps a few losses you will learn. Give people some time if you need to. If they make promises and fail to follow through, disconnect quickly. If you linger on and keep waiting, you will waste your time. Learn to recognize people and their intentions. Do not run to them like a baby at every phone call. Make them wait. Discuss things over the phone in detail. Assess the opportunity and then make a decision.

Learn to listen intently to what they say, read people, assess them and use your sixth sense if it's working. If someone promises you great offerings, see whether they deliver the goods. When someone says, "Oh, I will give you my next show," do not believe them unless you actually get the show. If someone asks you to meet them for a drink late in the evening, get a clue. No work happens over a drink in a pub at night. That is very clear. So stay away from such traps and stay smart.

Simply networking with anyone is not enough. Networking with the right people will assist you in getting new work. So focus on smart networking.

Recognize and welcome opportunity

In order for you to recognize opportunity you must stay alert. If your state of mind is fuzzy, you will most likely miss out on relevant work. When opportunity knocks at your door, respond to it and let it flow into your life. When I bought my first car in Mumbai, a beautiful Honda City, I went out for dinner to celebrate it with a few friends. After dinner, as we got ready to leave, we saw some salsa dancers in the lounge area. Intrigued we went inside. Some of the dancers were professional and one by one they kept asking us to dance with them. After jiving for a bit I stepped aside when suddenly a nice looking guy came up to me and said that he was a salsa trainer. He showed me some salsa moves and we got talking. He gave me his card. He happened to be an International distributer of documentary films. I told him that I worked as a freelance anchor. I did not think anything of this casual conversation and left the lounge soon after. The next day, this guy called me and informed that the French Embassy in Mumbai was hosting the 2nd French Film Festival for which they required an anchor. He asked me to meet the French ambassador and his secretary that same afternoon. He set up the meeting for me and fifteen minutes into the meeting I was finalized as the anchor and ended up doing the event. This happened so fast and just out of a chance meeting with someone over Salsa.

Opportunity can come in any form and it can come anywhere. You could bump into someone at the gym, at a party, at a bookstore, at an event or at the grocery story. Someone you may have met years ago might call you to offer work. You just need to be prepared and welcome opportunity.

Stay professional

Professionalism is another key ingredient for success. Being a thorough professional requires a mature and sensible mental framework. People gauge your professionalism when they see that you respect time and your commitment towards the work you have taken up. Being on time for your shows and events will enable you to gain respect. Once you reach the studio or event premises, utilize the time in getting ready for the show. Do not loaf around or flirt. Instead read through the script and make necessary changes. Discuss your look with the director and makeup artists. Try on the clothes given to you by the stylist. Ensure that you are physically and mentally in place ready to roll. Get to know the correct pronunciation of names you will be announcing during the course of the event. Try to rehearse your lines with your co–host to make the narrative crisper.

Put your cell phone on silent mode before you begin anchoring. If your phone rings while you are anchoring your show, many eyeballs will roll. You want to work in peace and distractions will not let you do so. You also will need to stay alert to goof ups on stage and quickly covering them up will gain you brownie points and in turn more work in future.

Professionalism also means that though you stay friendly with people you are working with, you do not get over-friendly. Stay away from gossiping or talking badly behind peoples back. This kind of behaviour is distasteful and will get you blacklisted. You want to stay in the good books of people. School-type gossiping might have been enjoyable in the past but won't serve any purpose now. Even if you do not fancy your director or their assistant, do not talk negatively about them to others in the workplace. Gossip is like breaking news and travels fast. Stay tactful and refrain from negative talk. If you portray a professional attitude at work people will respect it and not mess with you.

Keep conflict at bay

Conflict is a barrier to effective communication and is usually destructive in nature. Some people have a knack of creating conflict in a fraction of seconds. They enjoy drama and get bored in its absence. If you belong to this category, you have work to do. If you are the victim of drama and are often made a target, read on.

One of the key to getting long-term business from your client is to keep conflict at bay. When you work in vocations that require other people's assistance, it is best to maintain good relations. This is not always possible however, and there are moments when the situation instigates you to jump into an argument. There have been a few instances where I have run into conflict lovers. They do not need a reason to argue or blame someone. They can get started anywhere over anything. Such people need to be put in their place. There are gender wars as well at events and TV shows. Sometimes people of the same gender fight due to competition and try to one up each other. At other times there are issues between men and women due to ego and other issues. Whatever it is, conflict happens once in a while. We do not live in La-La Land where there is no conflict. Conflict is not always avoidable. However, one needs to manage it effectively and stop it from escalating. The question is whether you know how to manage conflict?

If you react easily to what people say, then you will need to understand this trait in yourself and make an effort to control it. Words can only harm us if we interpret them negatively. If we do not pay too much attention to sarcasm or negativity, it cannot get to us. In the world of work, prepare your mind to be at peace.

Keep the communication lines open with people and do not burn bridges. There is always an exception to this rule. Sometimes you may have to stand up against complicated situations/people, in which case you may decide not to work with them in future. That is fine but as much as possible try and sort out things amicably rather than getting into tiffs. Everyone has to deal with tough situations at work. Your behaviour and your attitude will either get you entangled into an argument or will smoothly get you out of one. Everyone has to deal with a little conflict or difference of opinion some time or the other, but then once it gets sorted out, let go.

Do not keep at it. Refrain from letting your ego get in the way. You need to learn how to say what you need to, logically and rationally, without disturbing your work. Remember, you are not a baby. If you have decided to step into the big bad world of work, learn to deal with things as an adult. You need to also learn to forgive those who have a habit of creating ruckus at work. Never take anything personally when you are in a professional setting. Being able to overlook certain things/people will be a blessing. Once you have identified people who are conflict-lovers, ignore them. In this case, ignorance will be bliss.

Answer your phone

There are a lot of people who do not answer calls from unidentified numbers. The one phone call you do not answer could very well be from a prospective employer who wants to offer you work. When you are in business, you must answer all calls. A missed call could become a missed opportunity. If you are wary of answering calls, you could keep two phone numbers – one that you give out to friends, your significant other, and to your family; and the other to work related folks.

Once I switched off my cell phone because I was getting random calls and went off to sleep. When I woke up and turned on the cell, I saw some urgent messages that were work related. One of the event companies I worked for needed me to do a short the next morning. However, by the time I saw the message and called them, they had already organized someone else. I lost on that work because I was not accessible to the client. Hence it is important that you keep tabs on who calls you and timely return their calls. You do not want to gain a reputation of not answering calls. Some people have a very bad habit of not taking calls even from their friends and by doing this a lot of times they lose out on relevant information and opportunity.

If you are busy or in a meeting, call the person back as soon as you get free; or send them a message that you will return their call shortly. If you can, then answer the phone and ask if you can call them back in a while. This kind of communication lets the caller know that you are reachable and will be available to speak in sometime. If it is something urgent, then communicate then and there to avoid any disappointment later. The bottom line is that communication lines should always be open. You need to stay alert and behave smartly in business and in life. You never know unless you listen and communicate. So get in the habit of communicating properly over the phone. Do not ignore calls unless they are from annoying telemarketers or pranksters.

Distribute business cards

Sometimes people that you meet may forget your name. When the mind is in ten different places, it is not easy to remember names of new people. A lot of meetings are quick and fleeting. In order for you to ensure that people remember you much after they have met you, give them your business card. Do not rely on people's memory to remember your name or your email ID. Your business card should be fuss free, simple and stylish. Most importantly it should have relevant information such as your name, your cell phone number, your email ID and your website (if you have one). You could also include what work you do – MC, TV anchor, Event Anchor, Video Jockey, etc. This will ensure that whenever there is a requirement for an area you specialize in, these people will contact you. In order to maintain your privacy do not put your home address on your card. You do not want random strangers knocking at your door.

Having an alternate phone number and email ID makes you easily accessible. If you are traveling and your phone is out of reach, people can email you. So give all this information on your card. People are too busy and will not hunt you down. If you are out of reach, they will call someone who is within their reach. Do not take chances.

13

Managing Things That Are Not In Our Control

So now that we have done everything in our capacity, what next? We have groomed, honed our skills and effectively networked. Now what? We may or may not get the kind of work we desire. We may or may not be content with what we get. We may or may not get the results we hoped for. The work is in our hands, the results are not.

There are thousands of people who are in line to get into anchoring. However only a handful few get work at any given time. Some things are beyond our control. Why do some people get work, get fame, and get assignments while others do not? Why do two people equally capable have a different success ratio? These are difficult questions and the answers to these are even more difficult to come up with. Some questions remain unanswered. Some answers remain mysterious. We just have to accept life's mysteries and come to terms with them. Whatever said and done, there are things which we cannot control yet we should know about them.

Luck and destiny

Though the concept of luck/destiny versus one's own effort remains highly debatable, we will delve into it here. There are all sorts of ideologies floating around in the world. Some people only believe in hard work. For them there is no such thing as destiny. They believe that if they put in their best effort, they will succeed. Then there are those that strongly believe in fate and destiny. They often give destiny the benefit of doubt and blame their stars when things do not go according to their wishes. Then there are others who believe in destiny to an extent and they also do not underplay the importance of their own efforts. They think that hard work and luck go hand in hand. All these are mystifying concepts and they are products of one's own belief system. They can be validated or argued. However, they remain forever mysterious.

Having said that, one cannot undermine the significance of destiny, luck, fortune or fate, whichever name you give it, as it is also essential for success. You need not run to a fortune-teller to seek out your destinies plan but you must understand that some things are not in your hands. Life can be puzzling and at times may present you with unanticipated results. If you have been slogging out for a long time, yet do not get work, take the cue. Perhaps you need to review your decision of working in Media. Understand that it is okay to change your decision anytime. This does not mean that you do not try.

Try and work towards your dreams but if you do not see results of your hard work manifest for a long time, review your decision. If you keep auditioning and do not get work, don't get disheartened. Do not jump to conclusions or blame your stars. That will not ease your trouble it will only make you cynical. You can change your course. When one door closes, another one opens. Not getting too much work or fame through your work is not the end to life. This is just your career choice, which can be altered at any time you choose.

Accept that everyone cannot do every kind of work. Your forte may lie in something else that you haven't yet discovered. Accept things gracefully. Do not compare yourself with others. Accept that each person has a different success ratio; they have a different journey and perhaps a different plan. You cannot imitate another individual's success or path, and nor should you. You have your own thing to do.

Dealing with disconnection and difficulty

Very large urban cities are filled with disconnected activities and places. There is too much happening. You get to see all kinds of things whether you are prepared or not. There is socio-economic discrepancy, there is a major divide between the classes and there is a lot of misfortune on the streets. You may be staying in the nicest area in town yet your day to day experience is not devoid of seeing adversity. Your environment makes a difference to your psyche. Whether you like it or not, you have to deal with everything that your city shows you.

In huge cities there is also an issue of disconnection. Most often there is no connection between any two places you may visit. At times you may even feel disoriented from such intense variation. When you go to an audition you view different types of people, get to see a different ambiance and a different setting. This is a created set-up which is often temporary. The moment you get out of there and onto your next destination you feel disconnected from the previous set-up. Urban life is extremely segmented. There is no continuation and hoping for a sense of belonging is a far-fetched aspiration especially for those who stay by themselves or with flat mates. The people who do not originally belong to the city they work or live in are more at risk of feeling disconnected.

In Mumbai, many young aspirants who audition day in and day out feel rather cut off and disjointed. There is so much incongruity that it is easy to feel out of place. One moment you are at an audition getting harrowed, another moment you are in your home away from all the hustle and bustle feeling relaxed, and the next moment you are at a five-star hotels' coffee shop feeling vibrant. The five-star culture is very different; it is a world in itself. When you come out of there you may see slums, you may see poverty. Then once you are back on the street trying to get from point A to point B, you cannot get through without getting hassled by street hawkers. There is too much disparity and a constant hustle.

Then there are the Rickshaw drivers and cabbies, which bring their share of trouble. The thieves and pick pockets in local trains pose danger that you have to deal with as well. You may be on television, you may be famous and you may be ultra-rich but you cannot completely free yourself from all these hassles. Just because you dress nice, wear stilettos and speak well does not keep pick-pockets and crooks at bay. The city spares no one. Everyone goes through the grind.

Even if you go to a beautiful high end lounge overlooking the sea, you will see people sitting on the beach watching you party. To see the less fortunate may take away your joy. You can ignore adversity, you can accept it; whatever you do, it remains in your face. When we go to a new city to work we have to deal with all these aspects as well.

Even with people, it is not as easy to form genuine or consistent connections. There is a lot of effort that goes into forming and maintaining friendships. People come and go easily because there are too many options; hence the value of friendship diminishes.

Study the city you live in and understand its nuances. Once you get a hang of the city you will expect less. When you expect less, you are disappointed less. Only expect what you can get out of it. Desiring too much peace or too much satisfaction won't help. Looking for water in the desert is futile. If you are in the desert, enjoy sand. Enjoy what the city offers you and leave the rest aside. Take care of yourself and protect your belongings. The city may not make you richer but it surely has the potential to make you poorer.

14

Little Dose Of Inspiration

Daily doses of inspiration are essential for everyone. When we are bombarded with various stressors in life and in work, we need to feel motivated and inspired. No journey to success is complete without inspirational tidbits. Living in a chaotic environment, being over-ambitious and raging to achieve can take a toll on the mind and body. Setbacks and disappointments can play havoc on the mind. Hence, keeping things in perspective is essential to one's well being. We need to relax and enjoy life's journey. Here are some tips to get you to stay positive while you strive to achieve worldly success.

Be kind to yourself

There is no need to get bogged down by self-imposed pressures. Setting unrealistic expectations for oneself is a sure shot recipe for disappointment. Understand that you are not some super human who should achieve everything over night. There is no such thing as overnight success. Many a times you will look at someone successful and assume that they have achieved success instantly. However, your assumptions will prove untrue after delving deeper into their lives. We only see the other persons' success; we do not get to take a peek at their day to day efforts. All success stories have a back log which the world does not get to see. We only see the fame, the glitz and get mesmerized easily. No success story however is as simple as it looks. Viewing others and setting unrealistic markers will only make you unhappy. Do not compare yourself to anyone else.

If you are out of work or going through low periods in your career, do not jump to conclusions. Taking things personally does not help. Putting yourself down does you no good. Instead understand that this business which you have gotten yourself into is very tough. There could be hundred reasons why you are not getting the kind of work you desire. Perhaps the market is down, perhaps the companies are on a cost cutting spree, perhaps their requirement is different than what you may offer, perhaps they get people dime a dozen. These are all reasons which have nothing to do with you. So stop taking things personally.

Putting unnecessary pressure on yourself will harm you, rather than help you. Maybe you have left your full-time job to pursue anchoring, maybe you have moved all the way from Canada or the US for a stint as a VJ, maybe you have run away from a small town because someone told you that you're hot enough to be on television, or perhaps your parents have given you an ultimatum that if you are not seen on television within a certain amount of time, they will get on your case. Whatever your story is, you need to keep things in perspective. Getting hyper won't get you work. So stay calm and stay kind to yourself. Buying into pressures and getting pulled in all directions will make your life hell. Give things time to unfold. Your psychological well being is most important and you will need to take care of your mind. A strong healthy mind will enable smart choices and will take you a long way. If you catch yourself dwindling, talk to someone, watch a movie or do anything which you enjoy. Everyone has a rough day once in a while, but remember that it too shall pass. If today is tough, there is always tomorrow which has all the potential to be amazing. This moment you may be feeling strange, but there is always the next moment when new opportunity may pay you a visit. Life is full of surprises and you never know when a miracle may unfold. So be good to yourself and don't lose hope.

Faith

We all need Divine Intervention at some point or another in our lives. Our faith is what gets us through difficult times. Faith, belief and hope are things that this world lives on. You too will need to have immense faith on your journey. Whatever be your belief system the fact remains you will never know all the answers. So get comfortable with the unknown. In this business, the greatest challenge is living with the unknown. You will not know many things, you will not know what your next project will be like, you will not know where it will come from and you will not know how things will go. You will need to keep the faith and think positively or else you will go crazy.

Positive mindset & the right attitude

The quality of our thoughts reflects the quality of our mind. If you think positively about yourself, your work and your environment, it may not make you successful but it will surely make you happy. Reacting negatively to circumstances, people or your work will only harm you.

A lot of people succeed because of their people savvy attitudes. On the first day of a show I was supposed to anchor, I met a woman at the studio, who said that there are three important things that a good anchor must have - Looks, Luck and the Right Attitude. This was the first tip I got when I began working in Mumbai. I do not even know the woman's name, nor will I be able to recognize her if I meet her again. Her words though registered in my mind. Our looks are genetically programmed and our luck comes under destiny's domain. However, the kind of attitude one carries is completely up to the individual.

Your attitude towards other people, towards your work, and towards yourself shapes up your success to a great extent. If you throw tantrums and show unnecessary attitude to people, they will get miffed and ignore you. On the other hand, if you show confidence, respect and stay positive, you will come forth as being a strong professional. If you are indecisive, untrustworthy or unreliable, then again you risk portraying an unprofessional image.

Attitude can be negative or positive. How you think will determine your behaviour. People can sense your attitude towards them, so watch out. A little tact goes a long way. Even when you decline work, do so politely. People will appreciate your politeness. If you complain about someone in a professional set up, it can be taken otherwise. Your attitude will reflect in your work. Having a positive attitude towards your work and your colleagues will take you through this rather inconsistent and rugged ride a tad smoothly.

Relaxation

Initially when you start working you may think that relaxing is a waste of time. You may have to run around all day to find work, meet people and audition. In this kind of hectic scenario leaves little room for relaxation. Some people do not even sleep enough, let alone relax. No matter what your current circumstances are, take some time out every day to do things which have got nothing to do with your work.

Find a hobby, play a sport, dance, walk in the park, read a good book or just listen to some soothing music. The idea is to get your mind off work and give yourself some down time. Give yourself a break every now and then. Deep relaxation will reflect on your face. You need to stay calm and cool in order to deal with the stresses that come with your lifestyle.

You can find many avenues to de-stress. Think of what makes you happy. Do things that enhance your joy. Engaging in fun-filled activities will add cheer to your life. You may like taking a walk by the seaside or you may like to play pool. You might enjoy painting or learning music. Find your de-stressors. Take time to indulge in your favourite activities, laugh out loud and breathe out your worries. There is a time for work and a time for relaxation. When you relax you let go of your insecurities and fears. Do it for your own peace of mind and for a better quality of life. Doing things that make you happy will help you stay healthier. Make a list of all things you love to do and start doing them. The time you spend enjoying life is priceless.

Be grateful

There is power in being thankful for what you already have. Blessed are those that get to follow their dreams. You have one life to live and you choose how you will live it. The work you will do; the place you will stay and the people you will befriend are all matters of choice. Make a list of all things you are thankful for, whether big or small. Giving thanks will make you feel good and look at all the positive things in your life. Having a habit of appreciating the good things in life will boost your morale and make you look at the glass half full.

If you are a constant complainer and think you have nothing to be thankful for, think again. A pessimistic outlook on life won't get you any form of pleasure. Everyone has something to be grateful for. What are you grateful for? What are you happy about?

One evening a friend of mine who lived in Washington D.C called me to share that he had finished graduate school and received an MBA. Delighted by this news I congratulated him and asked when the celebration was. He said, "Oh, I will be happy when I get a job." A few months later, the bugger got a job. I called to congratulate him and he said, "Oh, there is nothing to be so glad about. I need to buy a house and then I'll be happy." A year later, he bought a beautiful suburban home. This time I was apprehensive to ask him when the house warming was. While talking, he constantly complained about the mortgage and said that once he's done paying up he will think of celebrating. He paid up and moved up the corporate ladder, yet it was not the right time for him to celebrate. This is a true story of a friend who refuses to appreciate his achievements because he ignores what he achieves and aspires for what he doesn't have.

What is the point of achieving success – big and small, if you cannot appreciate and enjoy it? Stop postponing happiness. Don't delay your joy. Don't wait to get a project or a promotion to be happy. Be happy now, be thankful now. This present moment is all you have. Be grateful for all that you have and only then will you be appreciative of all you get.

Conclusion

In the business of television and events, nothing is certain. Nothing is permanent. Nothing is forever. If you understand and accept this fact from the beginning, you will save yourself from any kind of false hope. This business is gracious one day and stingy another. There is work one day and there is no work the next. There is fame when your show goes on air and there is the normalcy of life when you have no show on air. There is absolutely no consistency. Once you get this concept clear in your mind, you will be able to deal with life of a freelancer in a better way. If you take everything that happens or does not happen in your work personally, you are setting yourself up for huge disappointments. This is never all about you. There are a lot of people who decide whether to cast you or not in a show. There are a lot of factors that are considered before they zero in on an anchor. So do not take their decision personally or get demoralized. After twenty auditions you may get one show. After meeting ten event companies you may get to anchor one event. Or you may not get to anchor any. You need to become comfortable with not having work. This is a tough one to digest but it's the reality of working as an anchor in Media.

The lifestyle of freelance anchors is very different from those who work full-time. As a freelance anchor you may experience a wide range of thoughts and may even doubt your professional choices when there is no work. Be prepared for periods of dissatisfaction. In such professions there always remains a tug of war between the mind and the heart. You know you can do other things but you remain where you are because your heart tells you to follow your passion. If you decide to stay on this path, you must know how to manage it. Do not let the nature of your work affect other areas of your life. If you are not satisfied with freelancing, look at other business avenues. You could do something else on the side while you pursue anchoring. Stay the course if that is something you really wish to do but don't get stuck. This business has a shelf life so consider other options after you are done investing enough time anchoring. Having an alternate career goal, a plan B ensures that you stay encouraged and motivated to try something new just in case the current plan does not work out.

There is a pre-conceived notion among many people that anchors have it easy. They assume that all anchors need to do is look good and talk. Though looking good and talking are huge aspects of the job that is not all to it. Getting work is harder than doing the work. Though it looks easy, it is far from being easy. People think they have nothing at stake entering this business. They somehow feel that the investments are also low compared to other businesses. However, they do not realize that the time and effort which they would have to invest in this work is a lot more taxing than putting in big money. The monetary investments maybe low initially but the emotional and mental investments are very high. In a nutshell, this work requires a lot of grit, determination, mental strength, time, effort, hard work, luck and courage. If you choose this path, be prepared for a roller-coaster ride. Keeping a strong and balanced mind will get you through.